NICARAGUA DIVIDED

NICARAGUA DIVIDED

La Prensa and the Chamorro Legacy

To my good friends, Will and Faye, in appreciation, Patricia 1990

Patricia Taylor Edmisten

University of West Florida Press
Pensacola

The University of West Florida is a member of University Presses of Florida, the scholarly publishing agency of the State University System of Florida. Books are selected for publication by faculty editorial committees at each of Florida's nine public universities: Florida A&M University (Tallahassee), Florida Atlantic University (Boca Raton), Florida International University (Miami), Florida State University (Tallahassee), University of Central Florida (Orlando), University of Florida (Gainesville), University of North Florida (Jacksonville), University of South Florida (Tampa), University of West Florida (Pensacola).

Orders for books published by all member presses should be addressed to University Presses of Florida, 15 NW 15th Street, Gainesville, FL 32603

Photographs from *La Patria de Pedro*, 2d ed. (Managua, 1981), and *La Prensa Cincuentenario* (Managua, 1977) courtesy of *La Prensa*.

Quotations on pages 94 and 95 from Violeta Barrios de Chamorro, "The Death of La Prensa," *Foreign Affairs* (Winter 1986–87), are used with the permission of *Foreign Affairs* and the Council on Foreign Relations, Inc.

Library of Congress Cataloging-in-Publication Data

Edmisten, Patricia Taylor.
    Nicaragua divided: *La Prensa* and the Chamorro legacy / Patricia Taylor Edmisten.
        p.   cm.
    ISBN 0–8130–0972–3 (alk. paper)
    1. Nicaragua—Politics and government—1979–2. Chamorro
Cardenal, Pedro Joaquín. 3. Chamorro family. [1. *Prensa* (Managua,
Nicaragua)] I. Title.
F1528.E36   1990
972.8505'3—dc20   89–27505 CIP

CONTENTS

Dedicated to the Children of Nicaragua

ACKNOWLEDGMENTS

I owe my deepest thanks to my husband, Joe Edmisten, whose faith, flexibility, optimism, and love sustained me during the writing of this book, and to my son, Damian Taylor, who put up with my travels and frequent irascibility. I thank Frank Taylor for his staunch friendship, enthusiasm, and sensitive editorial work.

While in Nicaragua, Violeta Barrios de Chamorro opened her home to me as well as the offices of *La Prensa*. She enabled me to experience, to the degree that an outsider can, the Chamorro spirit and tradition. I hope that this book will suffice to thank her.

My heartfelt appreciation goes to the children of Pedro Joaquín Chamorro Cardenal: Pedro J. Chamorro Barrios, Cristiana Chamorro Lacayo, and Claudia Chamorro Jarquín who candidly spoke to me about their father, and to Carlos Chamorro Barrios whom I did not see, but about whom I learned from his loving family.

I am indebted to Pedro Joaquín's brothers and sisters: To Jaime Chamorro and his wife, Hilda, I say thanks for the hospitality of their home and for their confidence. I thank Xavier Chamorro for the tribute he paid his brother. I thank Ana Maria Chamorro de Holmann and her husband, Carlos, for their help with resources and for

Acknowledgments

their anecdotes of Pedro Joaquín. I also appreciate Ligia Chamorro's freshness and openness.

My admiration and affection go to the employees of *La Prensa* who took time from their busy schedules to share their impressions of Pedro Joaquín. *Muchas grácias* to Pablo Antonio Cuadra, Rafael Bonilla, Horacio Ruiz, Carlos Ramírez, Edgar Castillo (Koriko), and Melba Ligia Sandoval.

Thanks also go to Drs. Emilio Álvarez Montalván and Fernando Zelaya whose recollections of their friendship with Pedro Joaquín enhanced this work. I am grateful to Edgar Chamorro for helping me to understand the complex nature of the Nicaraguan political situation and to President Carlos Andrés Pérez of Venezuela for sharing with me the history of his friendship with Pedro Joaquín.

I extend my appreciation to Connie Works, Evelyn Grosse, and Lauren Booth of the University of West Florida for their skill and patience in the production of this manuscript, to the University of West Florida Press committee members for recognizing its value, and to the courteous and responsive directors, editors, and staff of the University Presses of Florida in Gainesville.

With this book I honor the memory of my mother and father, Dorothy and John Silke, who encouraged me to discover the world.

PREFACE

I went to Nicaragua for the first time in 1981 with a small group of professors and students. Oxfam-America, an independent development agency located in Boston, sponsored the group whose purpose was to study the food production policies of the new Sandinista government.

At the time of the trip I was preparing teachers to work with handicapped children. As a result of two years in Peru, where I worked with malnourished children as a Peace Corps volunteer, I was very interested in the relationship between malnutrition and subsequent intellectual and physical development. I was also interested in the political, economic, cultural, and educational patterns that permitted this human abuse. The Oxfam tour provided me with an excellent opportunity to see what the new Nicaraguan government planned to do to reverse these historic, unjust conditions.

In 1981 Nicaraguans were honoring the third anniversary of the death of Pedro Joaquín Chamorro Cardenal, publisher and editor of *La Prensa,* whose assassination was said to have triggered the revolution of 1978–79. I read reprints of his combative essays that urged social reforms to benefit the poor. His writings were strongly critical of the corruption of the Somoza regime.

Preface

When I returned to the United States, I undertook the translation of these essays. Later it occurred to me that the Chamorro story was a microcosm of Nicaraguan history, that it could help people understand the forces that brought about the Nicaraguan revolution as well as explain the struggle between Sandinista and anti-Sandinista. It might show that a mentality that uses only the Communist conspiracy theory is narrow, causing our foreign policies to be ill advised and harmful to the people we purport to want to help.

I returned to Nicaragua in 1985 after having first arranged to see Violeta Barrios de Chamorro, Pedro Joaquín's widow. I conducted my interviews with Violeta, other family members, friends, and employees of *La Prensa* in Spanish. The lengthy quotes that appear in the text are from these interviews and have not been published elsewhere. The translations of the *La Prensa* articles and the excerpts from Chamorro's books that appear in this work are my own.

Two of the Chamorro children are Sandinistas; two strongly oppose them. The ideological split within the Chamorro family is common in Nicaragua today. What is hopeful, however, is the overriding love that Nicaraguans have for their land and the hopes they have for its future—a future they want to determine. Nicaragua's salvation lies in this nationalistic pride. It transcends politics and can unite Nicaraguans just as it has kept the Chamorros a family despite their differing interpretations of Pedro Joaquín's legacy. Perhaps the actions taken by the Chamorros will predict what is in store for Nicaragua. If they keep before them Pedro Joaquín's dream of social justice and agree upon the means to achieve it, they will once again work together to bring peace to this suffering country. Maybe the rest of Nicaragua will follow.

The book is neither an exhaustive biography of Pedro Joaquín Chamorro nor a comprehensive history of Nicaragua. It is not a polemic against the Sandinistas nor a paean to those opposed to them. It is, instead, a true story of a prominent family whose lives reflect the complex nature of this wrenching transition period in Nicaragua. If I have succeeded in making U.S. readers more aware and compassionate in their responses to Nicaragua, if I have caused them to be more questioning of their government's policies, then I will have achieved my goals.

PEDRO JOAQUÍN'S FAMILY

Pedro Joaquín Chamorro Zelaya: Pedro Joaquín's father, who bought *La Prensa* in 1930, sought exile in New York when his newspaper was shut by Somoza García in 1944, and died in 1952.

Margarita Cardenal de Chamorro: Pedro Joaquín's mother, once active in the management of *La Prensa*.

Violeta Barrios de Chamorro: Pedro Joaquín's widow, the first female member of the revolutionary junta, who resigned because of political differences with the Sandinistas, codirector of *La Prensa*.

Jaime Chamorro Cardenal: Pedro Joaquín's younger brother, a top editor of *La Prensa*.

Xavier Chamorro Cardenal: Pedro Joaquín's youngest brother, director of *El Nuevo Diario*.

Ana María Chamorro de Holmann: Pedro Joaquín's older sister, a former editorial writer for *La Prensa*.

Ligia Chamorro Cardenal: Pedro Joaquín's younger sister.

Pedro Joaquín Chamorro Barrios (Quinto): Pedro Joaquín's eldest child, who was codirector of *La Prensa* after his father's death and in 1984 chose exile in Costa Rica, where he published *Nicaragua Hoy,* a counterrevolutionary newspaper supplement. He was later named to the contra directorate.

Claudia Chamorro Barrios de Jarquín: Pedro Joaquín's second child, a Sandinista who has served as Nicaraguan consul in Havana and ambassador to Costa Rica.

Cristiana Chamorro Barrios de Lacayo: Pedro Joaquín's third child, a subdirector of *La Prensa*.

Carlos Fernando Chamorro Barrios: Pedro Joaquín's youngest child, director of *Barricada,* the official newspaper of the Sandinistas.

THE SOMOZAS

Anastasio Somoza García (Tacho), 1896–1956: received military training in the United States; appointed director of the National Guard in 1933; reportedly ordered Sandino's murder in 1934; became president of Nicaragua in 1937 after a fraudulent election; assassinated by poet Rigoberto López Pérez in 1956.

Luis Somoza Debayle, 1922–63: older son of Anastasio Somoza García; president of Nicaragua from 1957 to 1963; credited with trying to liberalize Nicaraguan politics, making it impossible for close family members to succeed him; died of a heart attack before completing his term.

Anastasio Somoza Debayle (Tachito), 1925–80: younger son of Anastasio Somoza García; attended West Point; director of the National Guard; became president in 1967; resigned the presidency in 1979; assassinated in Paraguay in September 1979 at age fifty-four.

Anastasio Somoza Portocarrero (El Chigüín, The Kid), 1951–: son of Anastasio Somoza Debayle; born in Tampa, Florida; trained with the U.S. Army; first assignment with National Guard after 1972 earthquake; director of Nicaragua's Basic Infantry Training School; joined his father in Miami after revolution.

CHAPTER 1

MARTYR AND HERO

On January 10, 1978, Pedro Joaquín Chamorro Cardenal, stately, robust, fifty-three years old, made his customary visit to his neighborhood Catholic church before proceeding to the meeting he held every morning with the editors and managers of his newspaper, *La Prensa*. He had inherited the newspaper from his father and had directed it since 1952, using it as a personal front line against the Somoza regime.

This morning he traveled the same route he took every day, unchauffeured. If he was to die, he did not want to take anybody with him. Living with death threats had become a way of life for Pedro Joaquín and his family.

He had received a written threat at *La Prensa* only two days before. Perhaps it was sent in response to the critical editorial on the Cuban-owned blood bank that had recently appeared in the paper. Chamorro believed that the president of Nicaragua, Anastasio ("Tachito") Somoza Debayle, had a profitable business arrangement with Pedro Ramos, the Cuban medical doctor who had been soliciting the blood of poor Nicaraguans, giving them some food and money in return. Much of the blood was then shipped to the United States, where it brought a neat profit. To Chamorro this business was a further example of the Somoza style of draining Nicaragua's life blood, literally and figuratively.

These were perilous times in Managua, capital of Nicaragua and home of *La Prensa*. Each day brought reports of killings and kidnappings. In the United States, former friends of Somoza were withdraw-

1

ing their support. As revealed in a 1978 *Atlas World Press Review* interview, Chamorro did not mince words in encouraging that opposition: "I am very optimistic. I see the end of the Somoza dynasty. The majority of the people are against Somoza, except for the government workers. Somoza's regime is near the end because he lost support of the U.S. administration and public opinion in America and Europe. The newspaper now gives the truth about Somoza. He is a thief. He doesn't distinguish between his own interests and the interest of the state. When the dynasty disappears it will happen in Nicaragua as it happened in Spain when Franco died."[1]

Pedro Joaquín and his friend and codirector of *La Prensa,* Pablo Antonio Cuadra, had been invited to the American Embassy for lunch to discuss the growing opposition to Somoza. Chamorro was one of the most respected political moderates in the country and was thought the most likely to hold a key position in any new government should Somoza step down or be forced to leave. The embassy hoped to promote dialogue or political compromise between Somoza and the opposition parties. Cuadra said that "although the leftists were still weak at the time, Pedro Joaquín feared that, in the search for a means to oust Somoza, they would grab power."

An editor from *La Prensa* described to me what happened to Chamorro after he made his visit to church: "As he approached Avenida Kennedy, a busy thoroughfare near the outskirts of Managua, a man driving a Chevrolet rammed Pedro Joaquín's Saab from behind. The cars' bumpers locked, and the men inside the Chevy joined the driver of a Toyota approaching on Chamorro's left. Three men then opened fire with shotguns. They escaped in the Toyota, and Chamorro died minutes later, his body ripped by the blasts."

At *La Prensa,* Pedro Joaquín's elder son, who had worked there since he was a boy, was getting nervous. His father was always very prompt in starting the daily meeting. The son bore a striking resemblance to Pedro Joaquín when he was a young man and carried his father's first two names, preceded by the title "Quinto," or "Fifth," which meant that he was the fifth firstborn male throughout the generations to be named after the first Pedro Joaquín Chamorro, the first president of independent Nicaragua.

2

Martyr and Hero

A telephone caller notified the people at *La Prensa* that Quinto's father had had a terrible accident. Quinto rushed to the site. From all the traffic and commotion, he knew something horrible had happened. He parked as close as he could get to the area, which was jammed with people, and approached his father's car, seeing the shattered windows and bloodstained seats. The ambulance had just left.

Dazed and confused, Quinto headed for the Hospital Oriental. The staff at first was reluctant to admit him. Once he was recognized he was asked to identify Pedro Joaquín's body. It wasn't until Quinto left, carrying his father's blood-soaked clothes, that the people arrived— 40,000 of them. They had learned of Chamorro's shooting from the radio and by word of mouth, and they came to pray and wait, hoping that he would not die. After the hospital pronounced him dead, they escorted Pedro Joaquín's body to his home in Las Palmas, a green, shady neighborhood facing a pretty park in Managua.

Pedro Joaquín's wife, Violeta Barrios de Chamorro, a tall, slender, elegant woman of noble carriage, had been shopping in Miami with her daughter, Cristiana, at the time of the shooting. Cristiana, who resembles her mother in grace and beauty, was soon to be married. She and her mother were looking for trousseau items. While in Miami, word came from Violeta's brother-in-law, Jaime, that her husband had had a "serious accident." "No," Violeta responded intuitively, "they killed him." She called for Cristiana. "Let's go today, they have killed your father."

It is just over a two-hour flight from Miami to Managua. Violeta and Cristiana arrived home just as Pedro Joaquín's body was being taken to their home. It took five hours for the car bearing his body to arrive because of the crowd of people who had loved him. The event that Violeta and her husband spoke about so often before going to bed at night had occurred. Violeta described these conversations in a 1981 interview published in *La Prensa:*

> During his last years we spoke of death as if it were a natural thing. I, understandably, didn't want to speak about it, but one has to be a realist and see that we are all going to die one day, perhaps earlier than we think.

3

During the middle of 1973, in conversations with Pedro, I felt that we had to get our lives in order, not in the sense of thinking only about our happiness here, but in that other life, in that where we approach God, and of course we had to think of cemetery plots.

Since then our talks about death were as predictable as the prayers of a mass: "I am going to die," "I can die," "If this," "If that."

"Well, fine, if you are going to die, or if the two of us are going to die, we have to keep the eternal life in mind and also decide where our bodies are going to remain on this earth."

"You," I told him, "in Granada, because you were born in Granada, and I, in Rivas, because I come from there, but since we have formed our home together, we must be together at the end."

"Yes," Pedro told me, "but I am not buying land even though it looks marvelous."

"Well fine," I told him, "I am going to buy it."

"Yes," he told me, "but I am not going to have anything to do with those things. You do it."

On November 6, 1973, I bought a plot, no, two plots, side-by-side, to have them ready because of Pedro's uncertain and intrepid existence. Later I would say to him, "But, love, let's make a small crypt or a small tombstone or whatever."

"No, no, no," he said, "let the others worry about it if they should kill me beforehand." (I asked Eduardo Chamorro Coronel, the architect who did our house there in Las Palmas, to design the mausoleum.)

Later, during the evenings, I would hear Pedro speak of death with horrible persistence—he in bed, and I on the sofa, while he steadfastly repeated how the thing was going to happen and what would follow. Not until the day after they assassinated him did I truly realize that he was telling me all of that to prepare me, as though I were having a lesson, so that the blow would not be so hard, and yet it was so difficult that even today I am not able to adjust to it.

He insisted upon telling me how his burial would be, about what was going to happen in this country, and about the blood that was going to run when they killed him; about the enormous number of uncontrollable people on all sides, the flags of all of the political parties that would unite in that moment, the throngs in the streets and the flowers that would shower his funeral procession, and more flowers from the balconies. . . .

I, meanwhile, would tell him: "Pedro, you are crazy. God forbid that this should happen. I prefer to go before you. In addition, it is an enormous burden to hear what you are telling me—this is an incredible thing. No, no, no, God forbid, no!"

"Well," I told him then, "you will learn who I am."

Disgracefully, the moment that he was assassinated arrived. The tragedy was even more cruel for me because I was not here. I returned, and that night I saw coming through the streets the human sea that was carrying him, already a martyr. I thought that all of Nicaragua would not fit in Managua. My head was spinning with the same thought: the reality of all that he had foretold.

While we were keeping the vigil at *La Prensa* [Pedro Joaquín's body had been taken from the Chamorro home to the office of *La Prensa* where the Nicaraguans came to pay their last respects and offer prayers for the deceased], the National Guardsmen and the followers of Somoza arrived and threw tear gas and fired shots into the building. I then made the decision to take him with me to Las Palmas that next morning. I did not want more blood to flow. We took him in the *La Prensa* van to the Church of the Heart of Mary. The decision to bury him as soon as possible in order to avoid a holocaust took hold of me. Seeing the passion of the people caused by the assassination, hearing the cries of hatred and ire, I found the courage that only Pedro and God could have given me, and I stood upon a church bench and said, "Please, don't say any more; I ask you instead to sing the National Hymn of Nicaragua until Pedro is buried."

The people understood. It was the most beautiful and dignified event to be there, singing the National Anthem, with such respect.

People continued to cover the coffin with flowers and banners. "No," I said, "no banners. The best cover is the flag of our country—that flag in which I received Pedro—the Nicaraguan flag, the simplest and poorest of covers."

His Nicaraguan people and I are proud that Pedro Joaquín went to the tomb under that flag. Upon arriving at the cemetery, they continued to cover him with flowers. The people had climbed to the tops of mausoleums and threw flowers from there. They threw flowers from the balconies just as he told me they would. Before the first shovel of dirt was tossed, the man who was going to open the grave urged me:

"Take the flag, Señora."

"No," I told him. "Please put it into the coffin."

Pedro wanted to be buried with his flag. And there he is with it!

Pedro's burial was exactly as he had predicted it would be a million and one times. I would say to him, "Ay, love, you are a saint."

And he would say, "Why do you say that I'm a saint?"

"Well, yes," I assured him, "because persons who fight to do something for their country and who get rebuffed, but continue to struggle, are saints."[2]

Pedro Joaquín was buried in a crowded Managua cemetery. His starkly simple mausoleum occupies one of the two plots that Violeta had bought five years earlier. It has a tall, narrow, iron cross rising above it, and the inscription reads *"El nunca claudicó"* (He never wavered).

The assassination of Pedro Joaquín lit the fires of revolution in Nicaragua. Before his death, he had nearly succeeded in bringing about a coalition of political parties, the members of which had one goal in common: the ouster of Somoza and his tyrannical regime. Pedro Joaquín accomplished in death what he had not achieved in his lifetime: "The assassination . . . fanned tension into open conflagration. . . . This assassination, more than any other single factor, catalyzed opposition to the regime. It resurrected the ghost of the political assassination of Augusto Sandino* of 1934, and with it, the fears and outrage of a

---

*Augusto César Sandino, of peasant heritage, rose to be a commander in the Nicaraguan Liberal forces. He opposed the Conservative government supported by the United States. This led to his fight against U.S. military and political intrusion in Nicaragua and to his guerrilla struggle

frustrated people. It led to an unprecedented outburst of 'popular re-vulsion.'" So spoke Assistant Secretary of State for Inter-American Affairs Viron P. Vaky, in describing the effect Chamorro's assassination had upon the Nicaraguan revolution.[3]

It was as if the assassination was the last straw for the people. The upper class, hoping for a peaceful change, had been waiting for pressure from Washington that would have persuaded Somoza to step down. These wealthy people, who might have disagreed with many of Pedro Joaquín's ideas, still had a deep respect for him. They viewed his murder as a terrifying omen that their country was now beyond the brink, and if it was to reclaim any dignity and autonomy, they would have to join the cause to bring down Tachito Somoza. These people, too, had experienced economic losses due to his incursions into their own business fields. He had interests in many Nicaraguan concerns, and his power was such that he pressured people to do business with him or suffer the consequences. Additionally, the upper class believed that if Tachito stayed in power and a more democratic president were not found, the Communists would surely gain control.

With Chamorro's assassination, the small middle class lost all hope. He had fought for them. He believed that their enterprises were crucial to the economic health of the nation. He praised their hard work and saw the dignity in their struggle to provide for their families.

The poor also loved Pedro Joaquín. He had visited them in their barrios and had inspired them to fight for their rights. He had been their advocate on countless issues involving social justice. Many of their babies died before the age of five from diseases related to malnutrition. The poor were illiterate. Their housing was abysmal. Pedro Joaquín had written often on their behalf.

Time magazine described the upheaval that followed Chamorro's death: "For thirty years Chamorro had been a relentless critic of strongman Anastasio ("Tacho") Somoza and his family, who have ruled the nation for more than four oppressive decades. His death caused a political earthquake in Nicaragua."[4] The *New York Times* explained

---

against the U.S. Marines. See Gregorio Selser, *Sandino* (New York: Monthly Review Press, 1981), and Neil Macaulay, *The Sandino Affair* (Durham, NC: Duke University Press, 1967).

that "Mr. Chamorro's slaying has convulsed local society, with many Nicaraguans regarding the Government as ultimately responsible for the crime."[5] Carlos M. Vilas, a Nicaraguan sociologist, described the assassination's effect on the people in the *Latin American Research Review:* "It is evident that something in the heart and mind of the masses was definitely broken with the crime. For many people of the city, that death was the final proof—blatant—a brutal example that nothing was safe from the dictatorship; that there was no possibility of escape except through the elimination of the dictatorship by a direct action of the people."[6]

Although it was a natural reaction for Nicaraguans to blame Tachito Somoza for the slaying, now most would probably offer other theories as to who was responsible. Horacio Ruiz, longtime coworker of Pedro Joaquín's and later managing editor of *La Prensa,* told me that the person behind the plot has not been identified. "The assassination is still a mystery. Somoza saw a popular insurrection coming. The death of Pedro Joaquín would have inflamed the people. Somoza would have known the event would have harmed him." Ruiz reported that it was also unlikely that "the leftists would have done it in order to fuel the insurrection because Somoza would have known about it. He would have tortured that information out of them to protect himself." According to Ruiz, some people suspect that Tachito's son, also named Anastasio, was responsible, or that high officials in the National Guard, fearing Tachito was losing his grip on the country and was in ailing health, plotted Chamorro's death to eliminate what they perceived to be the greatest threat to their own longevity. Ruiz also described another theory, one that implicated the American Central Intelligence Agency (CIA): "They might have feared that Nicaragua was about to turn into a Communist country, and needed to create the conditions for a change." (Chamorro had by then been recognized in the United States as a key opponent to Tachito, and one whose death was likely to bring about a change in the government.)

In the March 1985 issue of *Soldier of Fortune* magazine, John Padgett blamed the Communists while absolving Somoza of the assassination itself: "Typically, culprits are found by assessing motive, ability and opportunity for committing a crime. Somoza certainly had the ability and opportunity to have Chamorro killed but he was not likely the culprit. In fact, he needed Pedro Chamorro. The publisher was his vocal and visible opposition, a known and identifiable figure that Somoza could use to prove he was running a democratic government. He could pick up a copy of *La Prensa* and wave it in the faces of skeptical U.S. Congressmen and reporters on fact-finding junkets in Managua to demonstrate his tolerance of political opposition. He could not be labeled a dictator if he allowed differing and diverse opinions to be published in the local press. And here was an example in *La Prensa*. Chamorro's continued survival and Somoza's tolerance of his tirades was the key to the vault of U.S. aid money for Nicaragua. No one knew that better than Antonio [*sic*] Somoza."

The Padgett article included an interview with Edgar Chamorro, second cousin to Pedro Joaquín, who in December 1982 became a director of the Nicaraguan Democratic Force (FDN, or contras), in charge of public relations.* When asked who killed Pedro Joaquín, Edgar Chamorro was reported to have replied: "You must ask yourself who would benefit from such a deed. Surely not Somoza or the United States. No, it was the Communists. We are certain. . . . You know, it was done so perfectly. . . . There had to have been KGB involvement. We Nicas aren't that sophisticated."[7] Edgar Chamorro amplified his *Soldier of Fortune* statement in an April 1987 interview with me:

> It could have been the KGB, but it also could have been the CIA. People who are involved in political conspiracies often have interests that overlap. Their approaches can be Machiavellian. Often one does not know for which side they are working. The differences become blurred, creating conditions for politicians to take advantage.
>
> The worst part is that no one is in control. It is almost irrelevant to know who is responsible because both parties have the same objective. The CIA also needed the last straw in order to remove Somoza. Somoza was framed because whichever group

---

*Edgar Chamorro left the FDN in the fall of 1984 because of forced recruiting and other abuses, according to the *New York Times* of September 12, 1985. Chamorro testified to the forced recruiting in an affidavit to the World Court.

9

or groups planned it knew that Pedro Joaquín's assassination would create conflict for the government.

Whoever masterminded his elimination from political life did so after a careful analysis of the two traditional alternating political forces in Nicaragua. I refer to those figures from Granada, the Chamorros and Sacasas, and to those from León, the Zelayas and later the Somozas. If the Sandinistas were to come to power, the representatives from the two clans would have to be eliminated; in this case, first Chamorro, then Somoza. Without the elimination of Chamorro, there would have been no elimination of Somoza. How sad it is that people play with the destinies of countries by way of political assassinations that change the course of history in order to achieve short-term goals.

By refusing to see the alternative that Pedro Joaquín offered, whoever was responsible led us into a blind alley. They ended any possibility of a peaceful solution. When there is no escape hatch, as was the case in Nicaragua, people explode.

The situation became uncontrollable. And then the people who were the most organized took power, and the only ones who were organized, had the commitment, political structure, and the mystique were the Sandinistas. They also had the loyalty of many of the people. The Sandinistas were probably surprised when all that power came to them.

The theory that initially got the most publicity, however, named Cuban doctor Pedro Ramos, who ran the blood bank with which Somoza was alleged to have economic interests. But the doctor, who proclaimed his innocence, had left for Miami shortly before the murder.

Jaime Chamorro, Pedro Joaquín's younger brother, admitted in his 1989 book, *La Prensa: The Republic of Paper,* that Dr. Ramos had sent the Chamorro family a private letter in which "he swore before God that he was innocent." The Chamorros did not make the letter public at the time because they believed the truth would come out in early investigations.[8]

As for Tachito's involvement, Jaime Chamorro believes that although Somoza might have had a substantial motive for killing Pedro Joaquín, the Sandinistas did also. "After all," Chamorro said, "the only ones who benefited from Pedro's death were the Sandinistas themselves."[9]

The Sandinistas annulled the findings of the first investigation and started their own proceedings against Tachito Somoza and his son, Anastasio Somoza Portocarrero, in August 1979. On October 15 both Somozas were indicted for their involvement in the plot to kill Pedro Joaquín. On June 18, 1981, nearly three and one-half years after the murder, a judge sentenced nine men (seven of whom were already in jail; two were at large) to terms ranging from eighteen months to thirty years. Although the Chamorro family seems convinced that the killers have been identified, they believe there are many unanswered questions regarding the Sandinistas' investigation, and they suspect a cover-up. They are sure that the killers "were and are ignorant of who really planned Pedro's assassination."[10]

The *Mexico City News* commented, "Whether Chamorro, director of *La Prensa,* was shot to death by supporters of the Somoza dictatorship or by extremists who wanted to make it look that way, the tragic result is the same, and the cause is the same—the venomous asphyxiating atmosphere of a dictatorship in which the exercise of freedom is almost tantamount to suicide."[11]

Gregorio Selser, a professor at the Autonomous University of Mexico, wrote of the assassination in an updated foreword to Pedro Joaquín's book *Estirpe Sangrienta: Los Somoza (Bloody Stock: The Somozas)*: "The system that Pedro Joaquín Chamorro fought killed him—the bloody dynasty that for more than four decades got rich on the hunger, backwardness, misery and desperation of the Nicaraguan people. It matters little that the hand which armed and paid the assassins was local or foreign. There was tacit complicity in the crime because since 1934, crime has been the convenient medium of the Nicaraguan government, regardless of who the victim has been. In the case of the journalist, Chamorro, like in that of Sandino, there was no improvisation, spontaneity or accident. The target was carefully selected and, even though it is possible that the reasons may not have been totally political, the result was the same: the greatest beneficiary was the bloody dynasty."[12]

Carlos Andrés Pérez, president of Venezuela from 1974 to 1979 (and reelected in December 1988), told me in a 1985 interview that "Somoza allowed the assassination to happen." Tachito desperately tried to convince Andrés Pérez that he was not responsible for the crime, but the Venezuelan president was adamant in his assertion of Somoza's responsibility—indirect, at least—for the murder of Pedro Joaquín, who had become Andrés Pérez's close friend when they were both in exile in Costa Rica in the 1950s.

Why was Pedro Joaquín Chamorro singled out for assassination? Would there have been a revolution had he lived? Many believe he might have been the logical person to replace Somoza had the Carter administration been more insistent that Somoza step down. One thing is certain: Pedro Joaquín predicted that he would be killed, and he knew the killing would be somehow connected to his longtime struggle against the Somoza dynasty. In a letter to Anastasio Somoza Debayle on January 18, 1975, he wrote: "I beg you to remember that Nicaragua is also ours, and so you should, if you have an ounce of patriotism, leave us in peace to organize and to rescue Nicaragua, even if it is done for future generations. And telling you this, I await with a tranquil conscience and a peaceful soul the end for which you have destined me."[13]

CHAPTER 2

TWO FAMILIES

Fruto Chamorro, Pedro Joaquín's great-great-uncle, was the first president of Nicaragua (1853–55). Three other Chamorros at four different times occupied the office: Pedro Joaquín (1875–79), Emiliano (1917–21), Diego (1921–23), and Emiliano again in 1926.[1] Although he never held political office, Pedro Joaquín Chamorro Cardenal had an even greater influence on Nicaraguan politics than did his ancestors.

He was born on September 23, 1924, in the colonial city of Granada, located on the shore of the vast, inland Lake Nicaragua. Pedro Joaquín was the eldest of six children. Their father "always seemed to have his head in books," according to one daughter, Ana María Chamorro de Holmann. Their mother, Margarita, "was the tenacious one—practical, serious." Ana María thought Pedro Joaquín took after their mother much more than after their father.

Pedro Joaquín had a passion for boating that lasted throughout his life. As a child he would sail on Lake Nicaragua, known for its freshwater sharks. There, with friends, he would "discover" the aboriginal god Tamagastad, as he pretended to make great archaeological finds.[2]

The young Chamorro knew all about William Walker, the North American freebooter who came to Nicaragua in 1855 at the behest of Nicaraguan Liberals who wanted to put down their traditional foes, the Conservatives.* Before going to Nicaragua, Walker had fought to

---

*The Conservatives—large landholders from Granada (the party to which the Chamorros historically belonged)—and the Liberals—merchants and small business proprietors from León and Corinto—have had a tradition

annex Alta California, which belonged to Mexico, to the United States. Achieving this, he took up arms against the infamous Mexican general Santa Anna, in an attempt to acquire Baja California for the United States.[3] Walker, accompanied by his band of mercenaries, was granted Nicaraguan citizenship and the rank of colonel.[4] He later declared himself president of Nicaragua and instituted the slavery that would soon be outlawed in the United States. The U.S. minister in Nicaragua visited Walker on behalf of President Franklin Pierce to advise him that "the Department of State, and especially President Pierce, wished to establish relations with his Government which, of course, enjoys recognition."[5]

For a short time Walker controlled the cargo and passenger ships that crossed the great Lake Nicaragua on which Chamorro sailed as a boy. In prison a century later, Pedro Joaquín reflected:

> There on the stage that one day would serve as the background of Nicaragua's tragedy against William Walker, I had my first notion of what "country" meant. Her pure land, wounded a thousand times by dominating tyrants; her simple peasants, my brothers, left illiterate by the ambitious, taught me to read the truth without letters. . . . The Indian gods, with their monolithic and barbarous beauty; the memory of the Spaniards; the virtue of honor, and the small sails that crossed the lake taught me to go honorably in life, without fear of the "southeastern," the cause of squalls and treacherous winds.
>
> I knew that no one had the right to snatch a people's destiny from them. I learned that my grandparents fought to liberate Nicaragua from William Walker, the freebooter. It was those ancestors with their heavy beards who agitated my youthful imagination from their picture frames hung in my father's library. . . .
>
> And later, my father, just and firm, kind and simple, impassioned by history and truth, more than once awaited my response when pointing to a mural of Granada and said: "Here fell Mateo Mayorga, or here fell Corral,* whom Walker had shot, accusing

---

of strife in Nicaraguan politics. Party names do not so much reflect an individual's "conservative" or "liberal" political behavior as one's heritage.

*Mateo Mayorga, foreign minister to José María Estrada, Conservative him of being a traitor." And later he talked to me about his family which had always rebelled against tyrants, and how his father and uncles spent years in jail wearing stripes and dragging iron chains until the tyrant fell.[6]

In 1930 Pedro Joaquín's father bought half the holdings of a newspaper that had its start in 1926. By 1932 he had bought out the remaining interests of *La Prensa,* becoming the sole owner.[7] Although the elder Chamorro was not a controversial figure, his newspaper was shut down in 1944 after his oldest son's involvement in the "Generation of the Forties," a group of university students who tried to prevent Anastasio Somoza García, then president of Nicaragua, from seeking reelection.[8]

Pedro Joaquín's studies at the Central University of Managua were interrupted by several weeks in jail for his participation in the demonstrations sponsored by the Generation of the Forties and because of his first street speech directed against the dictatorship. The students caused such a turmoil that Somoza García was forced not to seek reelection and instead named a hand-picked substitute. With *La Prensa* closed, Pedro Joaquín's parents sought exile in New York City, his father working as a translator and his mother as a seamstress. Meanwhile their son went to Mexico to study law at the National Autonomous University. His graduation thesis, "The Right to Work in Nicaragua," was used by some professors at the university as a resource work.

Pedro Joaquín visited the better presses while in Mexico City, learning whatever he could about printing, circulation, and administration.[9] He frequented the bullfights for diversion, studying the graceful movements of the matadors. (As a young husband and father, he would later entertain family and friends at picnics by donning a matador's cape and a three-cornered hat and challenging the local farmer's bull.)

---

head of state, was killed on orders from Walker. General Ponciano Corral was a Conservative commander who refused to accept Walker's authority and hence met death before a firing squad ordered by a war council composed of U.S. officers. See Gregorio Selser, *Sandino* (New York: Monthly Review Press, 1981), 14–15.

Nicaragua Divided

Chamorro returned to Nicaragua in 1948, when *La Prensa* was allowed to reopen, to collaborate with his father. In addition to editing, he introduced new graphics, better printing methods, and a completely different organizational structure. When his father died in 1952, Pedro Joaquín became director. (He had married Violeta on December 8, 1950.) Imbued with his energy and new expertise, *La Prensa* became the best newspaper in Nicaragua and could compare well with those from other Central American countries.

The newspaper's editorial policies changed considerably. Pedro Joaquín used *La Prensa* to portray the injustice of the Somoza García regime and the responsibility the Somozas had for the day-to-day misery in which so many Nicaraguans lived. He confronted the Somozas head on, and Nicaraguans rallied to buy his paper.

His management style reflected the influences of his upbringing: a Victorian sense of right and wrong, an unyielding discipline, a staunch Catholicism, and the legacy of ancestors who had themselves been agitators. Pedro Joaquín's longtime friend, Dr. Emilio Álvarez Montalván, in an interview with me in the Chamorro home, said that his friend "was very rigid in his values, very orthodox." His values would not allow him to stand by idly and watch the spread of corruption and unmitigated power engulf Nicaragua—a power that took its nourishment, according to Álvarez Montalván, from the United States of America. "Nicaragua gave birth to the dictators, but the United States incubated them."

That incubation began when four hundred U.S. Marines landed in Bluefields on the Caribbean coast of Nicaragua in 1909, at the request of Conservatives who had been trying to oust the Liberal president, José Santos Zelaya. The marines were sent to quell an expected uprising and to protect the lives and property of the foreigners in Bluefields. In 1912 an entire U.S. battalion disembarked at the Pacific coast port of Corinto to suppress a rebellion against a Conservative "figurehead ruler of the United States," Adolfo Díaz. By October 1912 there were 2,700 marines in Nicaragua. When the unrest ended, a force of 100 men stayed in Nicaragua to keep the peace.[10]

With the power struggle continuing between the Conservatives and the Liberals, the marines were again sent to Nicaragua on August 27, 1926, to protect the lives and property of U.S. citizens. In his book

Somoza and the Legacy of U.S. Involvement in Central America, Bernard Diederich writes: "When the United States became a world power after the Spanish-American War, it began to concern itself with territorial prerogatives in policy toward Latin America. The point was to keep European powers out of the area. While the ostensible reason for American intervention was to protect American lives and property and the rights of United States creditors, the main concern was maintaining security in the Caribbean and Central America. That meant keeping in power governments that were favorable to United States interest."[11]

The United States used Nicaragua's proximity to the Panama Canal as its justification for intervention. To protect the canal and American lives and property, the United States prepared an army that would "ensure democracy and constitutional order."[12] Although they stayed only briefly in 1926, the marines returned in 1927 to help Díaz maintain power, after he had been restored to the presidency unconstitutionally. In response to the presence of U.S. Marines in Nicaragua, the Mexican newspaper *El Universal* commented: "The United States has built a navy equal to that of the world's strongest sea power for the sole purpose of using this prodigious instrument to invade the coasts of Nicaragua. . . . The indignation of Latin American republics has been made all the greater by the web of spurious interpretations behind which the State Department conceals its aims, from the Under Secretary's propaganda about Mexico spreading bolshevism into Central America, to the most recent pretext that Nicaragua has been invaded to protect the property and rights of U.S. residents in Puerto Cabezas."[13]

In the meantime, Anastasio Somoza García, who had studied in Philadelphia and had an uncanny grasp of U.S. street language, returned to Nicaragua. There he succeeded in impressing Harry L. Stimson, who had been sent as a negotiator to Nicaragua by President Calvin Coolidge. Stimson hired Somoza García as his translator, and soon the ambitious Nicaraguan became known as "El Yanqui" because the people identified him with U.S. interests.[14]

Pedro Joaquín spoke of Somoza García's steady rise to power in *Bloody Stock: The Somozas,* the book he wrote while in exile in Costa Rica in 1957: "His career . . . was a child of the North American occupation of Nicaragua. The interventionists created a strong and efficient army, and at the end of their mission, they left it to him. . . . From this first step, he rose, little by little, until he had climbed the most remote peaks of Caesar-like power."[15]

Besides giving Nicaragua the National Guard and its thirty-seven-year-old director, the U.S. Marines also gave the country one of its greatest heroes, Augusto César Sandino. Sandino resented the imposition of a president by the United States and its influence on Nicaraguan politics. His rebellion, which had been organized to protest domestic political wrongdoing, grew to represent an anti-imperialist movement, which viewed the marines as the instrument of U.S. interventionist policies. (Six thousand of them came to Nicaragua in 1927 with orders from President Coolidge to "get Sandino, dead or alive.")[16]

Sandino fought the marines for five years. At first he suffered a serious defeat at Ocatal in northwestern Nicaragua when the marines used dive-bombing forays against the Sandinistas, followed by machine-gun fire. After this loss, Sandino and his men turned to guerrilla tactics. The rebel leader and his followers received tremendous support from the villagers, who provided them with food, shelter, and information regarding the enemy's location.

The U.S. Marines finally departed Nicaragua in 1933, having left behind, according to Diederich, "two deadly legacies: the National Guard they created and trained, and the man who was later referred to as 'the last Marine,' Anastasio Somoza García."[17]

On February 3, 1933, Sandino signed a truce in which he agreed that all but one hundred of his men would disarm in exchange for amnesty and land. He was gunned down by members of the National Guard one year later, after a visit to Juan Sacasa, the liberal president elected in a U.S.–supervised election. Somoza García allegedly gave the order but first checked with the U.S. minister. According to Diederich, "The minister hotly denied any involvement in the plot and the State Department issued a statement disclaiming any part in Sandino's death."[18]

On the evening of Sandino's murder, the National Guard, under Somoza García's direction, surrounded the Sandinista camp and machine-gunned its three hundred men, women, and children. In his book *Democracies and Tyrannies of the Caribbean,* William Krehm describes the extermination: "Somoza succeeded in eradicating practically the entire Sandinist movement. Nicaragua was swept clean of visionaries and prepared for a type of politics after Somoza's own heart. He later decorated himself for his accomplishments with the Cross of Bravery, Medal of Distinction, and Presidential Medal of Merit."[19]

Sandino became known for both his anti-Communist stance and his anti-imperialist position. His intense nationalism made him a logical hero to those who wanted Nicaragua out from under foreign intervention. The March 5, 1934, issue of *Time* described the phenomenon: "The death of Sandino, hero and symbol of Latin Americans' resentment against what they call 'The Colossus of the North,' sent a pang of sorrow and dismay from the Rio Grande to the Horn."[20]

With Sandino out of the way, Somoza García, still empowered by the National Guard, forced President Juan Batista Sacasa to resign in a coup he staged from fortresses in Managua and León in May 1936. Julian Irías was appointed acting president but lasted only three days. Somoza chose the interim president, Carlos Brenes Jarquín. Within a short time Somoza made himself the candidate of a newly formed Nationalist Liberal party. On January 1, 1937, having "won" the elections, he became president of Nicaragua. Washington's recognition followed.[21]

Somoza García assumed the roles of president and proprietor of Nicaragua as if he were born to them. However, it was the second role that eventually would bring about his assassination and that of his son and second successor, Anastasio Somoza Debayle (Tachito), who imitated his father so well.

Pedro Joaquín knew intimately the ways of the Somozas, having spent his adult life in combat with them. In *Bloody Stock* he describes the president:

> The characteristic flourish of the dictatorship of Somoza was his constantly aggressive attitude before the law. . . . Somoza and the law were contradictory, just like the terms "dictatorship" and "democracy." He was a tyrant in every sense of the word, a man who pretended to be above everybody and who only obeyed the dictates of his own emotions.
>
> . . . His vice, in the execution of power, knew no limits. For him, the essential was to win in everything—to command—even

19

when those commands were contrary to reason. While he amassed an immense fortune, that none of the other capitalists of the country could have ever imagined, and while he monopolized all of the resources of the Republic for himself and his children, he was also meddling in smaller ventures: His baseball team couldn't lose, his purebred horses had better win at the race track, and his prize cattle had better receive awards at the agricultural fairs.[22]

William Krehm interviewed Somoza García about reported abuses after the student uprising that sent Pedro Joaquín and his family into exile in the forties. Somoza answered in his fluent street English: "I wanta treat everybody good, see! But if they don't come across, well let them remember that I got an iron fist under my silk glove. I know that they complain that the glove is too thin, but I pray God that it never rip."[23]

Somoza García's style was not without a certain humor. In *Bloody Stock,* Pedro Joaquín gives examples of Somoza's warped sense of humor in dealing with his critics. He writes of a man who had declared that "it had been impossible to work in Nicaragua without the consent of the Somozas, and that the only path for honorable people was mendacity." When Somoza read that declaration in a local newspaper, he decided that the speaker should be taken by force to spend some time in the asylum for beggars. On another occasion Somoza ordered that a patrician gentleman, respected for his civic pride and valor, be detained at the asylum for the mentally ill for having the audacity to say that "Nicaragua, governed by Somoza, was a country of lunatics."[24]

In 1948, impatient and disgusted with the Somoza style of government, Pedro Joaquín founded the National Union of Popular Action, known as UNAP. The organization's motto was "In the Service of Truth and Justice," a phrase that later appeared above the masthead of *La Prensa.* Cofounders included Dr. Álvarez Montalván and other friends from the Generation of the Forties, most of whom had become upper-middle-class professionals. They were united in their desire for social revolution. According to Pedro Joaquín, it was "an attempt to establish a Social Democrat or Social Christian Party."[25] The party had a short life, but many of its members participated, to some degree, in the 1954 plot to overthrow Anastasio Somoza García, according to Álvarez Montalván.

Given his daily exposure to Somoza's abuses by way of the people who sought help from *La Prensa,* it was not surprising that in 1954 Pedro Joaquín became a member of the "Frente Interno" (Internal Front). The Frente, according to Charles Ameringer, author of *The Democratic Left in Exile,* was to cooperate with former members of the Caribbean Legion, a group made up of those who had been forced to spend time in exile because of their struggle for democracy and social reform in the Caribbean region.[26] Their efforts in the 1954 rebellion to oust Somoza García failed, and the "silk glove" quickly slid from his hand.

Only a few of the conspirators escaped. Many were captured, tortured, and murdered. Pedro Joaquín, imprisoned as a result of his involvement, later testified that Tachito hanged a collaborator by his testicles in order to get him to confess.[27] Three months after Pedro Joaquín completed his two-year term, the second year of which was under house arrest, he was arrested for conspiracy in the assassination of President Anastasio Somoza García.

On September 21, 1956, the Somozas were taking part in a whirlwind of fiestas held in the university city of León. The president was in high spirits—merry, solicitous, always the "patrón." Between dances, as he was looking at a newspaper article that a friend showed to him, shots rang out. The general dropped the paper, fell backward, and gasped, *"Ay mi Dios"* (Oh my God).[28] Within seconds Somoza's bodyguards shot the assassin, the poet Rigoberto López Pérez.

A U.S. helicopter from the Canal Zone brought the dying Somoza to Managua, where the commander of Walter Reed Army Hospital had been sent to attend him. Also present were the chiefs of surgery and orthopedics and an anesthetist from the zone.[29] Somoza died one week later. President Dwight D. Eisenhower sent the following message to Nicaraguans: "The Nation and I personally lament the death of President Somoza of Nicaragua as the result of a cowardly attack by an assassin who was killed some days ago. President Somoza constantly emphasized, both publicly and privately, his friendship for the United States—a friendship that persisted until the moment of his death."[30]

Pedro Joaquín and Violeta, unaware of what had occurred, were

21

intercepted on their return from a party on the night of the assassination. Pedro Joaquín was arrested. He was not alone: "There were gentlemen in their seventies, politicians, and people who had never been militant in opposition parties; some were half-dressed, others barefooted, and the rest in pajamas, wrenched from their beds to feed the rising tide of military vehicles headed for the jails."[31]

In addition to the familiar Nicaraguan faces, Pedro Joaquín recognized a U.S. citizen called "Rip" by the Somozas, either because of his appearance or the similarity of his last name to that of "Van Winkle." Rip had attended the same party as Pedro Joaquín on the night of his arrest. Three days earlier *La Prensa* had published a letter on Rip's role in the Somoza government by the wife of a distinguished Nicaraguan journalist who had "disappeared." She addressed her letter to U.S. Ambassador Thomas E. Whelan and asked him if U.S. citizens, according to the laws of their country, could participate in political and police operations in Nicaragua. The letter clearly linked Rip with the disappearance (p. 29).

In *Bloody Stock,* Pedro Joaquín had more to add: "Whelan was a good friend of the Somozas. He was photographed with the family on as many occasions as possible. He traveled with them, dined with them in their private reunions, and helped them to govern. He undermined any U.S. goodwill by always siding, in his reports and attitudes, with the Somozas. On the other hand, Van Winckle was the organizer of the Security Office of our country so it was logical to complain about his role in the sinister kidnapping of the journalist" (p. 29). So Pedro Joaquín was not surprised, on the night of his arrest, to find Rip at the door of the Office of Security. "Walk this way," he said. "Yes," Pedro Joaquín replied, calling him a "pirate and filibuster." "Van Winckle did not answer, but his presence in that place, and his notable activity in everything that was occurring there, did not leave the remotest doubt about his position. He took part in the interrogations of many persons, and witnessed many of the horrible scenes that hundreds of Nicaraguans lived in those days, without losing his nationality. He was a great teacher; one can't deny it—a formidable technician in the art of driving people mad and wrenching lies, as well as truth, from the prisoners" (p. 30).

Two Families

Pedro Joaquín, like others on a long list the general had kept, was a logical suspect in Tachito's mind. The two younger men had been enemies since each could remember. Tachito charged that *La Prensa* had kept up a steady attack on his father that he would not tolerate. Pedro Joaquín described the Somoza dynasty as "permanent parasites, stealing and corrupting everything in sight."[32] Now Tachito had his hour with his enemy of long standing, whose continuing resistance to the remaining Somozas was to be sorely tested in the *cuarto de costura*, or "sewing room," of the presidential palace.

Pedro Joaquín followed a uniformed man through a maze of corridors, saw maids coming and going about their duties, and was led through a small door that opened to the sewing room. Upon entering, he heard cries coming from within. He knew that he was soon to be tortured, yet this knowledge brought him some relief:

> I was certain that they were going to torture me. When one is sure of the inevitability of something, he has the same sensation as a sick man who finds himself in the operating room: The sooner, the better. Perhaps it does not hurt as much as they say. From that moment, all of the normal world that one has just left disappears. It becomes small and almost unreal because man is concentrating on himself alone and begins the great fight for integrity, honor and life. (pp. 68–69)
>
> . . . In that place I must have passed the most horrible six days of my life. . . . For six days the interrogations went on interminably; the blows fell on every part of my body. I especially remember those that fell under my waist. . . .
>
> They would apply brilliant lights to my eyes that exploded the brain after first burning my pupils and the skin on my face. If I closed my eyes, I would be dead. They robbed me completely of sleep. . . . Heavy eyelids that cannot give in to gravity; weakened muscles that I must control; chaotic thinking that I must not allow to totally disintegrate so that consciousness remains, pathetically vigilant, at the feet of another. (pp. 72–73)

Within this circle of brutality, the other prisoners treated those who were to be tortured with the greatest respect and with the most touching consideration. As a man would be called from his cell, another would offer him a cigarette that had been concealed from the guards; another would extend a towel that might help to keep him warm in the cold, damp quarters; still another would assist him in buttoning a shirt. Then the order would come: *"Vamos, vamos, apúrese, hombre"* (Come on, come on, hurry up, man). The victim would leave with the guard. Those in the cells would pray for their colleague. "It is always the same, like when one is being dressed for the coffin, like when one is preparing for a solemn and painful occasion, only during these times the clothes are few, invariably filthy, and always the same," wrote Pedro Joaquín. "I have been a part of many of these scenes. Among those who stay, there is at first a silence, and later, they begin to speak of the absent one, no more or less than one would speak of a dead man at a vigil" (p. 39).

"The youngest son of the dynasty," as Pedro Joaquín always referred to Tachito, who was still head of the National Guard, had a keen interest in the progress of the publisher's "treatment." He visited the prisoner in the sewing room. Dressed in spotless khakis, medals polished, his fat belly was the only incongruent feature in his martial presence. Sometimes he would shout at his prisoner, impatient with him and others who insisted they were telling the truth, when to him they were all liars. At other times Tachito would lower his voice and smile, intimating what had happened to others. Furious with Pedro Joaquín's denials of involvement in the assassination of his father, Tachito yelled, "There . . . there, where you are standing, have passed many who have sworn to me by Jesucristo that they are innocent, but they were lies. They were all guilty!" (pp. 74–75).

The journalist clung to his denials, and the six days passed as though an eternity. For him the absence of a sense of time was additional torture:

> There are people who can suffer many kinds of physical pain without faltering, but man, because of the transitory nature of his body, cannot support an eternity that has no end. It is not a question of valor or cowardice. It is something sociobiological that can only be understood by one living in a place where hours

have no meaning; where "tomorrow" does not exist, nor afternoon, nor evening; where pain and anguish do not have confinements because they exist at all times, mixed in with the food and the diversions of the executioners. . . .

The mind empties itself and becomes as blank as the wall before one, and then they begin to write on it what they want: "The General is very good. Perhaps you did not realize, but tell me now, frankly, what harm did he do you so that he was killed like a dog?"

And one starts to think that perhaps they are right; that the man who ordered the attack on the mine in which hundreds of peasants were killed was good; that he who embraced Augusto César Sandino hours before having him shot was good. . . . Why shouldn't he be a good man, like others, with children, grandchildren, with normal family worries? (pp. 80–81)

At times Pedro Joaquín inhabited a cell from which he could see the Somozas' exquisite garden with its sparkling fountain and exotic birds. Although birds were often found in the gardens of the wealthy in Nicaragua, wild animals were not. Somoza García had received lions, tigers, and panthers as gifts from several heads of state. They lived in cages within the garden—and so did some men:

The lion paced and so did the man. Man and beast in contiguous cells, in the same cage, divided only by thin bars, both matched—intelligence and instinct in an indescribable tableau, behind the same bolt.

In addition to the man paired with the lion, there were two others put into the panther's cage and two more in my corridor, and others at the end of the garden, immobile, like white statues, like mummies because of the lack of food and the abundance of suffering. (pp. 87–88)

In the garden Pedro Joaquín frequently saw Luis Somoza, the new president of Nicaragua, with his younger brother, Tachito, accompanied by their wives, friends, and children. "The innocent children carried their dolls and toys almost in front of the cage where the man lived with the lion. On more than one occasion, small visitors, children of the servants of the palace, passed before us, with mixed expressions of surprise and pain written on their faces" (p. 89).

Rigoberto López Pérez, Somoza García's assassin, would not have wanted any of this brutality to befall the men taken as suspects and conspirators. He acted independently. Before leaving for Nicaragua from El Salvador, where he had been living, the poet left this letter for his mother: "Although you have never known it, I have been a part of the resistance to our country's lamentable regime, and in view of the fact that all efforts have been useless in an attempt to restore Nicaragua to freedom (or perhaps bring it to her for the first time), I have decided, even though my companions will not accept it, to try to be the one who begins the end of this tyranny. If God wills that I should succeed in my effort, I do not want anyone else to be blamed because it has all been my decision" (p. 138).

López Pérez undertook the task knowing he would die. He did not do it for glory. He believed that with Somoza García's death would come the opportunity for fundamental changes in his land and imagined that a general rebellion would complete what he had begun. The young poet took out an insurance policy on his life for his mother's benefit, and before his departure he attended a baseball game. He had no interviews with political leaders and looked only for Somoza (pp. 137–38).

Unable to believe that their father's death was caused by one man acting alone, Luis and Tachito Somoza subjected Pedro Joaquín and many others to the wearying travesty of the Nicaraguan Military Courts after they had first received "treatment" in the sewing room. The Somozas had had careful instruction in the use of the system of military courts from the U.S. Marines early in the century. Pedro Joaquín, who ultimately came before Somoza's courts on three different charges, wrote that the United States left their codes but not their moral structure. This court system, "used in 1933 by the U.S. Marine Infantry, never was approved by the Nicaraguan Congress. It was not law in Nicaragua, but the Somozas applied it to their enemies— civilians and military—indiscriminately" (p. 111).

When Pedro Joaquín came before the court, hurriedly set up in the house of one of its members, the interrogators tried repeatedly to get him to confess to conspiracy in the assassination. The writer, whose body had been weakened by blows, managed to stand tall and take the questioning with dignity. He firmly denied involvement in any conspiracy and for this was given "the opportunity to amplify his declaration" by the court. This "opportunity" consisted of a return to the sewing room.

It wasn't until Pedro Joaquín's torturers had nearly obliterated his will that he falsely confessed to having known of a conspiracy and not having reported it. This confession, extracted by the most hideous of methods, became Pedro Joaquín's shame—the only one of which he ever wrote.

The confession, set down on paper in the sewing room, was not used as evidence when Pedro Joaquín returned to the court. By this time he had recovered his determination and continued to deny his part in any conspiracy. Returned again to the sewing room, he faced Tachito, who threatened: "You're laughing at me, right? But know one thing: that from here only God's providence can save you. And if you think that your declaration can absolve you, think again. . . . From the door of this jail, you will not take three steps" (pp. 107–8).

At last and reluctantly, Pedro Joaquín confessed before the court to his knowledge of the plot to kill Somoza García and named a man whom he greatly respected as the individual who apprised him of it. He uttered the words of the confession as though each was traveling on a last breath. Now he would be allowed to have a lawyer and sleep. (He was later to deny his confession in public and seek forgiveness from those who believed in his integrity.)

The military court found him guilty of having knowledge of a rebellion without reporting it. After spending six months in jail, Pedro Joaquín was banished for forty months to the small village of San Carlos del Rio on the southern shore of Lake Nicaragua.

Pedro Joaquín's experiences in prison represent only one story in the maniacal spiral of vicious treatment imposed on prisoners. A close and older friend of his was forced to remain for forty days in a triangular "tomb" in which he could only be in a prone position. He saw no light and had no human contact. Others were trussed and repeatedly immersed into the cold waters of a well, also known as the "thermal

27

baths." Here they were brought to near asphyxiation to make them more cooperative.

Witnessing the grisly manifestations of Somoza power, Pedro Joaquín often pondered on its source. He believed that it emanated from a simple fact: The Somoza empire was entirely centralized within the context of family and the resources that surrounded it. They lived in a separate and armed city:

> Within a circumference of 500 meters from the center of their residence are: a battalion protected by 45 Sherman tanks, the only artillery that the country has, an infantry battalion armed with the latest weapons and a company that patrols the streets of Managua when there are disturbances. It is the center of all telephone and radio communication of the army and has the primary warehouse for military supplies, the offices of Investigation and Security, and all the arsenals—all operated by one master key.
>
> Above their own rooms, they have anti-aircraft guns; in the kitchen sleep no fewer than 60 selected soldiers, armed with carbines, ready to mobilize themselves as a personal guard, directly commanded by officers who are the most intimately linked to the family. (p. 117)

In jail Pedro Joaquín had plenty of time to consider the historical animosity between himself and the Somozas. This animosity harkened back to grade school where he and the sons of the assassinated dictator shared the same school bench. "Their father was already head of the National Guard, and mine, owner of *La Prensa*. . . . Later, in the same halls of the Pedagogic Institute of Managua, when their father began to enrich himself in full view of the country, I expressed my doubts about the General's businesses, and our arguments turned violent. Tachito never forgot it, and so he reminded me of that old antagonism when I was being tortured in the 'sewing room' of his palace. Ever since those early times there has been a struggle, sometimes mute and at other times open, staged from the two positions that we held in Nicaragua: He, the prince, born in the cradle of power, owner of fabulous businesses, always trammeling the rights of others and trying to preserve the empire created by his father. I, fighting with an independent newspaper that never gave in to the threats or to the cajolery of power" (p. 236).

Although Pedro Joaquín said he never conspired to kill Tachito's father, he understood what Seneca professed: "Tyrants do not die, they are killed" (p. 114).

CHAPTER 3

REBELLION AND RELIGION

In March 1957, after having served six months in prison, Pedro Joaquín was sent to the southern town of San Carlos del Rio. San Carlos is situated next to Lake Nicaragua near where the lake empties into the San Juan River, which serves as the border between Nicaragua and Costa Rica. He was taken to the commander of the local guard and was ordered to find his own housing, not to make appointments, and to present himself to the guard three times a day.

To Pedro Joaquín, San Carlos resembled a setting from the type of film he adored, Westerns. But the town had the advantage of being on the lake and, unlike Westerns, in San Carlos the people spoke only of fishing. Abraham, an elderly black man with a white beard, was famous for expounding his theory of how Lake Nicaragua's famous sharks get there—they swim up the San Juan River like salmon. Wondering whether or not this theory would stand up, Pedro Joaquín toyed with the idea of researching it, if only to pass the next forty months. He decided whimsically that he would need someone to cooperate at sea level so that newborn sharks could be marked. Then he would try to catch any that arrived at the lake.

Apart from the fishing, there were few other diversions in San Carlos. A rickety ship, *The General Somoza,* arrived once a week. Then there was López, the eccentric pilot, who twice a week brought in Protestant preachers along with some weary adventurers from the interior. López always approached the airstrip from the reverse direction, leaving only two hundred yards between the end of the strip and the lake.

Meanwhile, Violeta, unwilling to be separated from her husband for forty months, went to San Carlos, having left her children in the temporary care of her mother-in-law, Margarita Cardenal de Chamorro, with whom she and Pedro Joaquín had been living. Violeta's plan was to find a house in which they could be together for the term of the banishment. Her husband, however, had different plans. They would escape to Costa Rica.

In many ways, Latin Americans prepare for Easter more carefully and celebrate it more fervently than they do Christmas. Pedro Joaquín took advantage of this situation to flee San Carlos on Holy Saturday. Tachito Somoza, still head of the National Guard, had stated that it was precisely because he hoped that the prisoner would attempt an escape that he was sent to San Carlos—to provide the needed justification to kill him. The knowledge of this statement did not dissuade Pedro Joaquín.

As night fell, he guided Violeta, who wore slacks under her skirt and carried a missal and rosary, to a dark place near the wharf where they scanned the night for the man who was to take them to safety. Violeta saw the boatman first. In his excitement Pedro Joaquín must have signaled too loudly because the man warned, "Be quiet, we're going to a free world—to one without fear."[1] The skiff soon entered the dark waters of the San Juan, and the threesome were enveloped by the night sounds. As the river widened, its passengers repeatedly turned around to see if they were being followed.

As they progressed, Pedro Joaquín reviewed the river's history as if trying to become one with it. The Spaniards discovered it when they were exploring Lake Nicaragua, known then as the Mar Dulce (Sweet Sea) because of its fresh water. The river was part of the first interoceanic route and has remained important for most of Nicaragua's history. Commodore Cornelius Vanderbilt's steamers plied the same waters in the middle of the last century, carrying passengers and cargo from Greytown (now San Juan del Norte) on the Atlantic coast to the port of La Virgen on the western shores of the lake. From there mule trains would complete the journey to San Juan del Sur on the Pacific coast.

31

In the mid-1800s travelers from New York to San Francisco regularly took this route.

It was also William Walker's territory and served as his supply lane. Ironically, after Walker colluded with Vanderbilt's former partners to gain control of the route and the steamers, the commodore helped to supply the Central American forces that would oust Walker.

Now Pedro Joaquín was using the river as his escape route. He worried about being missed in San Carlos. If he were, it would not be long before the guard, in their powerboats, would be rushing headlong to retrieve or kill them. Violeta prayed. Because of the tranquil waters and the sameness of the lush, opaque foliage on the banks, it seemed as though they were hardly moving.

After three hours they entered a tributary of the San Juan where they had to row against the current. They passed an estate that belonged to the Somozas and heard the piercing cry of dogs. Their anxiety mounted. All about them lizard-headed fish, called in Spanish *gaspar,* leapt out of the water, soaking them in their descent. Except for the sound of the fish they startled, the journey grew more and more silent. "It was only adorned by the sounds of the forests, the whisper of Violeta's rosary and the parting of the water by the skiff."[2]

They eased by a hacienda that had its own wharf where National Guardsmen were known to take off and apprehend those dealing in contraband. A brilliant beam broke the darkness, scanning the black river. The boatman urged Pedro Joaquín to row as silently and swiftly as possible and asked him if by chance he had a revolver. He did not. Eluding the searchlight and the guardsmen, they continued downstream until they saw the glow of lights from the town of Los Chiles, near the spot where they would disembark, in the country where they would remain in exile for the next two years—Costa Rica.

They walked the last leg of their journey. Violeta asked what they were approaching in the darkness. When told that it was an airport, she ordered that the lantern be turned off for fear of their being shot. Smiling, their guide informed her, "Señora, here they don't shoot anybody."[3]

Pedro Joaquín and Violeta started new lives in San José. He found employment at the *Prensa Libre* (*Free Press*), a San José daily, and devoted much time to writing *Bloody Stock: The Somozas,* in which he intended to expose the cruel farce of the regime of Anastasio Somoza García "to benefit those who fight against tyranny in Nicaragua and other American countries." In the preface he also wrote that he wanted to "explain to the children of those who were assassinated by the Somozas, the reasons behind their parents' sacrifices."[4]

Pedro Joaquín could have made enormous contributions through his courageous articles (when they were not censored) without undertaking additional life-threatening activities. He could not merely inspire, however. He had to be what his pen encouraged, and so he became one of the authors of the rebellion of 1959.

He organized the Nicaraguan resistance movement in Costa Rica against the first heir of Somoza García, Luis Somoza, and his brutal brother, Tachito. With the help of powerful friends like Carlos Andrés Pérez of Venezuela and others of the democratic Left, Pedro Joaquín managed to procure arms for his movement.

Pedro Joaquín and other leaders of the democratic Left even went to Cuba to solicit arms from Fidel Castro, who became premier in February 1959 and had been supportive of their efforts. However, the Nicaraguans parted from Castro because they believed he had designs for implanting his own movement in Nicaragua—one that would serve his own interests and whose development he would control.

Chamorro considered himself to be a civil coordinator rather than a military leader. He worked with other civilians in a search for the economic resources that would bring, by way of revolution, social and political reform to Nicaragua. Young men came to his door seeking information or bearing news from Nicaragua. Eventually Pedro Joaquín decided that he needed to bear the same risks as these young men who wanted to fight for their country. To do otherwise would have caused him shame.

For one and a half months Pedro Joaquín and others trained for their military return to Nicaragua at La Llorona, a beautifully rugged beach area on the western coast of Costa Rica. Once in Nicaragua they intended to link up with resistance forces there. Pedro Joaquín would command one "battalion."

On May 31, 1959, 110 men walked the craggy beach to the spot where their DC-46 Curtis Commando awaited them.* They flew above Puntarenas, the beach known for its volcanic black sand, and headed toward Lake Nicaragua. The first unit, under Chamorro's leadership, was dropped off at Los Mollejones in the Department of Chontales, east of Lake Nicaragua. The plane later returned to Costa Rica for the second group, which was taken to Olama, northeast of Managua, in the Department of Matagalpa. These men were part of the first air invasion anywhere in Latin America. After two weeks of steady pursuit by the National Guard, air bombardments, and machine-gun fire, Pedro Joaquín was forced to surrender and was again imprisoned.[5]

Five months later, Violeta received the letter that her husband wrote to her the day his unit surrendered. He had put it with his identification papers so that if he should be killed, Violeta would know that she had always been carried in his heart—even to death. Later the letter would become evidence against him:

> Now I am in the hands of God. He is grand and powerful. He makes miracles, but if He decides that my time has come, I will have your image and your spirit before me. Your goodness and love will carry my soul to the next life.
>
> Forgive the suffering that I have caused you. Forgive my coarseness. It hurts me to have to leave you and my children, but what am I to do?
>
> My love, yesterday there was a ferocious bombardment and the Virgin kept me safe. I have faith that she will guide me, but if she decides to call me to her side, forgive me and remember me.
>
> Tell your children that they, and other children like them, are my country, for whom one must suffer, sometimes unto death.[6]

Although Pedro Joaquín had feared that the invasion was premature, he feared even more that radical Nicaraguans under Castro's sway would preempt them with an invasion from Cuba.[7] About the defeat Chamorro wrote: "No one thought that our lone force of one hundred

---

*The plane belonged to the Costa Rican National Airlines (Aereolineas Nacionales de Costa Rica). The pilot was an employee of that agency.

men was going to defeat four thousand National Guard. We were one piece of the machinery, and we completed the first part of our mission. The disaster came when it was discovered that of that machinery, ours was the only piece that had moved" (p. 172).

Pablo Antonio Cuadra, a well-known Nicaraguan poet who had assumed the directorship of *La Prensa* during Pedro Joaquín's imprisonment, commented on Chamorro's role in the rebellion during my 1985 interview with him: "Pedro Joaquín did not have confidence in change through prolonged force. He hoped for a quick 'golpe' [coup] to get rid of Somoza and then wanted a provisional government set up until there would be elections. The internal situation wasn't ready. This failure made him suffer much."

Cuadra remembered the letter he received from Pedro Joaquín while he was in jail, depressed, embittered, weakened, his heart profoundly sad. Cuadra responded: *"El fracaso no es más que el éxito al revés"* (Failure is no more than the reverse of success). "Now all your 'friends' have left you. Tomorrow they'll join you, but these are not really your friends. Be thankful for the happy lesson you've had at such a young age." Explaining why Luis and Tachito Somoza did not have Chamorro killed for his participation in the rebellion, Cuadra remarked, "They didn't kill Pedro Joaquín because he was among the best of Nicaragua, and there would have been a terrible uproar."

From prison Pedro Joaquín began his book *Diario de un Preso* (*Diary of a Prisoner*). Visitors would smuggle out the scraps of paper to Violeta, who eventually pieced the work together. In 1961 he wrote an epilogue to it that included the following remarks on the rebellion: "We thought that we could attempt the military defeat of the regime in order to achieve the establishment of a new system of government. . . . We believed that our action would be contagious, and that through it, the Nicaraguans would achieve a new social structure that would completely eliminate the exploitative and monopolistic system under which we had lived. We went to Olama and Mollejones with the idea of implanting in Nicaragua a system disposed to the belief that there is no achievement that deserves to be called 'progressive' if it does not benefit the poor."[8]

Cuadra, in interpreting Chamorro's misperception of the situation, noted that "Pedro Joaquín had an illusion that a small army could make Somoza fall because of his lack of popularity. He forgot Somoza's machine, the National Guard."

The defeat of the rebellion weighed heavily on Pedro Joaquín. More than anything else, the lack of internal support must have been devastating to him. He was not a man for whom surrender came easily. Perhaps his convictions about truth and justice were so deeply rooted that he could not conceive that his countrymen, while espousing revolt, would lack the courage to act upon their words. Pedro Joaquín needed to justify his surrender to himself, even though by surrendering he had saved many lives. He wrote in his diary, "Those who have never had the opportunity to surrender, never had the valor to rebel" (p. 11).

September 14 is a national holiday in Nicaragua. On this day the people celebrate the 1856 battle of San Jacinto in which Nicaraguans, commanded by General José Dolores Estrada, defeated William Walker and his North American mercenaries. On that holiday Pedro Joaquín was getting some sun in the prison's courtyard. Overhead flew planes—the same kind as those that had bombed him and his men three months earlier. Several Nicaraguan Air Force "Mustangs" had shelled them for five hours. Chamorro asked himself if this was the use the United States government intended for its planes and the pilots it had trained (p. 30).

There had not been trials for treason in Nicaragua since Walker's time. The new trials recalled those of the Walker era, when proceedings were held against the Nicaraguan patriots who defended their land and would not accept the American's claim to be their president. The military court was similar to the one Pedro Joaquín had faced after the 1956 assassination attempt. This tribunal, however, made use of many telephones. Journalists were allowed to attend, but their reports and cables were censored.

According to Nicaraguan law, the tribunal had a hierarchical structure. At the head was the "Autoridad Convocadora" (Convening Authority); whoever served in this highest position had the power to decide such matters as recesses, substitution of judges, and other related matters. In this case the position was held by General Anastasio "Tachito" Somoza Debayle, chief of the National Guard. Pedro Joaquín believed that the judges regularly phoned him for confirmation and advice.

Just before the tribunal's decision, Pedro Joaquín had a dream that he described in *Diary of a Prisoner:*

Last night I dreamed that a tribunal, composed of seven men, called me to come before them, saying, "Citizen Chamorro, you are condemned to search for a country." They were dressed in enormous coats of khaki material, full of shining buttons, with small black skulls in the middle. One had two skulls on his shoulders . . . he with the big eyeglasses who told me with studied affectation, "You may go now to search for your country at the market."

After, I felt them shove me into a long and dark corridor where I heard strange and excited voices. "Fresh countries," shrieked a woman. "Countries, countries for sale, on installments, with no down payment. A country for sale, with television, two bedrooms, refrigerator, and a salary of 3,000 pesos a month."

I was very confused, and since I did not clearly understand the announcement, I stopped to hear better. In that moment, the dark corridor became lighter, and where I stood a window opened. In it appeared a fat, pink, old man with a red lamp in his hand. He shouted at me, saying, "Fresh countries, delicious, with television, refrigerator, and automobile. Countries with the 'Somoza' brand—model, 1959, with shock absorbers, with clergy, and without any obligation to worry about the welfare of the country. See for yourself, in this aerodynamic model of a country all inconveniences that can bother an owner have been removed. It has an electronic isolater that separates its owner from the worker; a magnetic switch that disconnects the conscience; and a marvelous code that cancels every idea of justice—a troublesome complex from which past generations suffered. Buy this new model of a country. You only have to pay in installments, surrendering your will—that known as 'free will,' and some cents' worth of honor. But in exchange for that, you will have a television, automobile, the switch for your conscience, and money—much money."

The old man became quite tired from his harangue, and his red lamp suddenly illuminated the showcase of a small shop in which had been placed various models of what he was trying to sell. "No," I said, horrified. "I will not buy that."

Then, in the long hall, there was an interminable din of screeches and shouts of every kind. I desperately ran and kicked the red bricks of the store that sold countries, with my muddy boots, while behind me were all the members of the tribunal who, without my having realized it, had been witnessing the discussion with the old man. They were fencing with enormous wooden swords.

At last they grabbed me and conducted me to the room in which they had earlier convened, and placed me alone before their table, surrounded by chairs with red backs. Behind the table there was an immense portrait of a smiling man who smoked a cigarette with a good-natured and happy air.

"We are going to read the decision to you," they told me, and he who was seated in the middle, swelled his horrible voice with a microphone and shouted, "This court has found Citizen Chamorro guilty of the crime of treason." (pp. 189–92)

Pedro Joaquín woke up suffocating. He boiled a little water for coffee and pondered the dream. One hour later they took him to the tribunal that would judge him. He found many similarities between the members of the actual tribunal and those of the dream. There was, nevertheless, a notable difference: Instead of skulls, these men were adorned with small metal stars.

Pedro Joaquín and his friends broke into laughter whenever they heard the testimony against them. They laughed even when they heard their sentences. It was as if they saw absurdity in everything and that laughter was the only means by which they could express their despair. Pedro Joaquín described this situation in *Diary of a Prisoner:*

We laughed at ourselves, at our own men, at the youths of our small country buried in disgrace, at the government, at the revolution, at our children, our fathers, our history, and at our future. The judges laughed, and so did the prosecutors and the guards who watched us. We all laughed evil laughs, and we felt pleasure seeing how we had sunk with the country. There were grand guffaws, full of shame and pregnant with defeat. And the laughs become stronger and longer.

Why did we do this? Perhaps because we are trained, educated, and almost molded to do it. This is our school, our way of life, of loving, of doing business, of playing, and of dying. The joke, the laugh, the guffaw, the disdain for the human person that bursts forth, is the typical attitude of Nicaraguans of this period. . . .

We are nearly the perfect product of the Somocista era. The youth become completely cynical before becoming men because of so many humiliations. . . .

The tragedy occurs before maturity. The humiliation accompanies us from the cradle, and the corruption awaits us in primary school. It is not the corruption of alcohol or of vagrancy; it is other, worse—a prostitute more ugly than prostitution. . . .

We have rebelled. . . . We have fought against the humiliation and against the lessons of the old official prostitute. We have called her "liar" to her face when she has wanted to teach us that to be a patriot is to be rich. . . . We have wanted to fight against her with sticks, words and rifles, but she has conquered and has returned to humiliate. (pp. 178–81)

The tribunal found Pedro Joaquín guilty of treason and condemned him to nine years in prison. Even though he knew that he would not receive a fair trial, he had not realized how severely the label "traitor" would wound him. To him the word meant "to sell," to deliver one's country up to an enemy. Certainly "traitor" could not be attributed to someone who was willing to give up his life to achieve an honorable and just government. No, such behavior would describe a patriot.

On the way back to the jail on Tiscapa hill, Pedro Joaquín and the other prisoners passed Violeta among the wives who had been waiting for news outside the walls of the military installation and the "Hall of Justice" where the trial had taken place. Christmas was just a few days away. From the hill Managua spread out before them, a carpet of colored lights.

Pedro Joaquín entered his cell, hearing the creaking of the door latches and the clanking of the iron bars as they closed him off once again from his family, friends, and work. He folded his clothes and put them on the box he used as a table and then lay down on his cot. Three times he had returned to this place, wearing the same striped clothes, sleeping on the same bed, feeling the same fatigue. Three times he thought that he must revive. He remembered a close friend's words: "A failure is like a crucifixion; no one can revive without having first been crucified." Then came the thought, "This is the end, but perhaps it is also the beginning" (p. 227).

During his years in prison, Pedro Joaquín dwelt frequently on the themes of Christianity and communism and on the irony of being labeled "traitor and Communist." He did not fail to recognize, however, that the motivation behind his own political movement and that of the Communists was, in part, similar. In *Diary of a Prisoner* he wrote:

> I have fought against Communists. My companions and I were deceived by the cunning manipulations of their chiefs who placed obstacles between us and our revolution. . . . They are and continue to be our enemies, but it is necessary to say that the same cause which produces them (at least in Nicaragua) is the same that produces movements like our own.
>
> . . . The oppression from which we suffer propels us to construct a new public structure. In that, we are the same, and both of us are right—we and the Communists—because all of us are Nicaraguans, suffering the same oppression and the same injustice. Nevertheless, we differ in that while they attempt a revolution that destroys the first revolutionary of humanity, Christ, we attempt another that comes close to Him, humanly and politically speaking. (p. 154)

Pedro Joaquín was not soft on communism, nor was he fond of blind anticommunism:

> There are few concepts as empty and common as pure anticommunism because it signifies nothing. He who adopts it as his only coat of arms has no thoughts of his own and only knows how to oppose foreign or strange thinking.
>
> . . . I am not a Communist because I am a Christian. But

I admit that I do not hate those I'm supposed to hate in order
to do my duty and appear a true democrat. . . .

. . . When one loses faith in the world's justice; when one
experiences persecution in the guise of that which is convention-
ally considered good, honorable and respectable; and when at the
same time one does not know Christ because no one has shown
him Christ, one is forced to give in to the temptation to subvert
the order of things as they exist, and help create another order,
that, in the case of communism, may be the most brutal, but also
the most sincere. (p. 153)

Pedro Joaquín believed that revolution was inevitable in
Nicaragua—that it was just a matter of time—but he was deeply dedicated to the concept of "Christian revolution": "Revolution is necessary
not because the Communists say it is, but because revolution is necessary when there is no roof, bread, liberty and work for the majority
of people. It is also necessary that the revolution be Christian because
only in this way can respect for individual dignity be maintained within
community life."⁹

According to his youngest sister, Ligia, as a student Pedro Joaquín
carried a tiny statue of the Virgin Mary in his bookbag or in his
pocket. As a grown man he didn't begin his workday until after his
visit to church. Violeta said "he felt protected by God." In prison he
tried to find consolation in his personal faith, gaining strength from
the realization that Christ, like him, dealt with duplicity and cruelty:
"God has permitted that they crucify us. He has made us choose between submitting to lies and servility, or drinking the bitter cup of lone-
liness and sadness. . . . Christ did the same thing before Herod and,
in this way, taught us that he did not have to adapt to the exigencies
of hypocrisy. Christ knew that he would be crucified, and so then why
argue with Herod?" (pp. 93–94).

Pedro Joaquín loved Bishop Fulton Sheen's book, *The Life of
Christ*. In it he found material for the comparisons he used when writing about the key ruling figures in Nicaragua. He found in Herod "a
common prince, equal to any Latin American dictator." He wrote that
"Pilate has lived in Nicaragua for many years, reincarnated, with slight

41

variations, in the presence of many American ambassadors." He continued his comparison:

> Pilate, a kind of "American Ambassador" in Judaea, understood that Christ was innocent, but in spite of having the right of deciding life or death over the Judean people, applied the principle of non-intervention, and turned Jesus over to the dictator, Herod. Pilate's fine political tuning dictated that approach in order to preserve the international prestige of Rome whose soldiers were openly occupying Jewish land, but without meddling, as modern rules of non-intervention dictate in the internal politics of an occupied country.
>
> . . . Herod knew that this "non-intervention" only existed in Pilate's imagination. Roman intervention was a reality, given its power. . . . The Romans breathe by the law and are the inventors of justice. Their imperial eagles cover the world with swords and lances and with millions of edicts and decrees. They are strong and just, have military bases everywhere, do business with, and respect the mores of the peoples they rule. They represent western civilization. (pp. 207–8)

CHAPTER 4

IN THE SERVICE OF TRUTH AND JUSTICE

In June 1960, one year after his trial, Pedro Joaquín was released from prison in a general amnesty. He had been accused by President Luis Somoza of organizing the rebellion with the help of Fidel Castro—help the Nicaraguans had refused. (Castro was soon to defeat rebels who would begin their invasion of Cuba from Nicaraguan shores with Luis Somoza's encouragement.)

In *Dictators Never Die*, leading Latin American journalist Eduardo Crawley wrote that Luis Somoza had wanted Pedro Joaquín and his men captured alive because he did not want to evoke sympathy for the rebels among the wealthy families to which many of the young men belonged. The president even charged the rebellion's leaders with seeking the deaths of their troops in order to evoke hatred toward the guard among the general population.[1]

Luis Somoza was astute in his recognition that Communist-baiting was a popular activity in the United States. He knew, too, that the U.S. government preferred that he be more of a democrat than his father. Luis Somoza called his own administration a "bridge to democracy." So while he labeled everyone who called for change a "Communist," he also ordered the general amnesty in which Pedro Joaquín was released and announced, to Tachito's chagrin, that the constitutional ban on reelection would be enforced, as would the law forbidding the candidacy of the incumbent's blood relatives. Pedro Joaquín interpreted these changes: "Luis wanted to get rid of it all. Not the country or his properties, of course; he wanted to inaugurate a period of transition after which his family, while remaining the most important family in the land, would not wield power directly."[2]

Press censorship was eased. The ten journalists from *La Prensa* who had been arrested after Somoza García's assassination were released. Horacio Ruiz, who continues as managing editor and whose tortures were described in *Bloody Stock,* was also freed.

The loosening of the chains of censorship, combined with a move to reduce cronyism in the business world, stood in stark contrast with the recent past. Chamorro wrote in *Bloody Stock* of Luis Somoza's father: "Somoza García's newspaper business enjoyed privileges while those of his enemies had been nearly driven to extinction. His newspaper operated out of public buildings like the national stadium. He impeded reporters from other newspapers from obtaining news releases from official sources before his own people had access to them. He authorized, at government expense, foreign travel which included trips to cover international sporting events. He used the government's maintenance shops to repair his machinery and required public employees to buy subscriptions and take out advertising, while he jailed, threatened, beat and exiled those who attacked his system of government."[3]

To the foreign press, Somoza García presented a very different image. He was a charmer, wining and dining them, telling them risqué jokes, and even allowing them to check out selected rumors of torture. In *Bloody Stock,* Chamorro described the kind of torture that leaves no marks and the parading of those who suffered this torture before the foreign press:

> "You know," would begin a journalist, innocently, "we want the truth. Have they tortured you?"
>
> "No."
>
> "We desire to be fair. What has been your situation while detained? How have you been treated?"
>
> "Very well."[4]

Never naïve about the regime and not moved by Luis Somoza's gestures, yet not wanting to miss an opportunity to help forge a democratic Nicaragua, Pedro Joaquín took to the airwaves from 1960 to 1966 with the spoken equivalents of the essays that appeared each afternoon at five o'clock in *La Prensa*. In 1962 he published *Diary of a Prisoner* about his involvement in the 1959 rebellion and his subsequent imprisonment and torture, followed by his book *5:00 P.M.*, based on his editorials and published in 1963. He was elected to the Board of Directors of the Inter-American Press Association (IAPA), which had continued to monitor his situation while he was in prison and pressured the Somozas for his release.

In September 1963 Pedro Joaquín and *La Prensa* launched a literacy campaign supported by radio, schools, the universities, and the Ministry of Education. The newspaper published more than 100,000 primers and admonished: "We have arrived at the conclusion that one who does not know how to read has the right to insist that one who does read, teach him, and that the latter should not refuse such an obligation. . . . One who does not know how to read is like one who cannot see, and it is necessary to take the blindfolds off our brothers. If every one of us who knows how to read would teach one who doesn't, we would be doing an immense and incalculable service for Nicaragua."[5] Luis Somoza attacked the campaign and Chamorro's part in it. According to a 1981 *La Prensa* publication, *La Patria de Pedro (Pedro's Country)*, Somoza and his followers began to sabotage the campaign with every kind of obstacle and pressure.

Meanwhile, unable to succeed himself in 1963, Luis Somoza, with his brother's guidance, urged their National Liberal party to nominate René Schick, a former personal secretary of their father's and minister of education under Luis, for president. The Conservative party nominated Fernando Agüero, who demanded that the Organization of American States (OAS) be allowed to send observers to the elections—a request that was denied. Instead Agüero was put under house arrest when he tried to rally support for his cause. Luis Somoza called upon the rubber-stamp Nationalist Conservative party to come up with a substitute opponent who dutifully lost to Schick in the elections.

President Schick was not the yes-man the Somozas expected. He prosecuted a guard member who was found responsible for murder, and he promoted business development within the private sector that was independent of Somoza's interests. He even spared the life of Carlos Fonseca Amador, one of the original founders of the Frente Sandinista (Sandinista Front), which had been organizing and gaining strength in the rural areas. (An eternal flame now burns next to Fonseca's monument in the central plaza of Managua. He was killed in a skirmish with Tachito Somoza's troops in 1976.)

Exasperated with his brother and frustrated by Schick's reforms, Tachito announced that he would seek the presidency after Schick had completed his term in 1967. Schick died of a heart attack before the end of his term, however, and the interior minister, Lorenzo Guerrero, completed the term, receiving his orders from Tachito.

Incensed by Tachito's unconstitutional power play and aware of the diverse sources of opposition to him, Pedro Joaquín led the struggle against the younger Somoza's grabbing of the presidency. He united the Conservatives, Christian Socialists, and Independent Liberals who again nominated Fernando Agüero as their candidate.

Agüero attracted some 60,000 people to a political gathering on January 22, 1967. In his book on the Somozas, Bernard Diederich described the opposition as carrying signs that read "No more Somozas" and "No more assassinations." Agüero wanted a national strike to force the government to guarantee electoral safeguards. The crowd started moving toward the national palace, hoping that the National Guard would join them in a move of solidarity against the Somozas. Instead the guard fired upon the demonstrators. Forty were killed, one hundred wounded.

Pedro Joaquín was not among the demonstrators. According to Diederich, he had been taken from his home, without a warrant, the day before. He told newsmen that whenever the guard searched *La Prensa,* they would "plant something and say that they have found arms in that place. They're not difficult to predict; they always play the same simple games." The guard occupied the offices of *La Prensa,* and there was no newspaper until February 3.

Chamorro was taken to the prison known as "El Hormiguero" (The Anthill) where he was kept in a cold bath for the first twenty-four hours and frequently felt a gun at his temple. At one point a guard grabbed his testicles to "find out what size they were."[6] To justify his imprisonment, "evidence" was found at *La Prensa* implicating him in a plot to overthrow the government through terrorist activity. Forty-five days after his arrest he was released without having voted in the elections that made Anastasio Somoza Debayle president of Nicaragua.

Luis Somoza died before his brother was inaugurated. The reporting in a *New York Times* article was sympathetic:

> Luis Anastasio Somoza Debayle was credited with sincere efforts while President of Nicaragua from 1956 to 1963 to liberalize the strong-man regime his father, Anastasio Somoza, had imposed on Central America's largest country. . . .
>
> The two brothers worked smoothly to keep control after their father's assassination. The efforts "increased the family fortune to an excess of $100 million," according to an estimate in the *Worldmark Encyclopedia of the Nations*.
>
> . . . Early in his administration he acted to bar the next presidential term either to himself or any family member in the fourth degree of kinship. But in June, 1959, the brothers had to put down a rebel force from Costa Rica.
>
> For six months, Nicaragua was under a suspension of constitutional guarantees. "My father," Luis Somoza asserted, "often warned me that you cannot feed too much meat to a young baby, and now I know what he meant!"[7]

With Luis dead all the Somoza wealth went to the new president. Crawley reported in *Dictators Never Die* that Tachito owned one-fourth of the arable land in Nicaragua, an area equal to the size of neighboring El Salvador, and that one-half of the registered land in Nicaragua was his, officially at least.[8]

Pedro Joaquín needed to get away from the political shambles of Managua. Still an avid boatman, he traveled with a small group of close friends down the San Juan River, from the town of San Carlos (from which he escaped in 1957), past the forgotten villages on its banks to Greytown on the Caribbean. Except for its notoriety during the gold rush years and its association with Vanderbilt, Walker, and those who wanted to build a canal through the country, Greytown and the southern coastal zone had been ignored by the government and the vast majority of Nicaraguans. Pedro Joaquín called attention to the previously ignored coastal area in his 1967 book, *Los Pies Descalzos de Nicaragua (The Unshod of Nicaragua).* He considered the poverty there to be a security concern and thought it deplorable that the region was not contributing to the development of the nation: "All the pirates, buccaneers, and filibusters of past epochs and present have been, and continue to be, very aware of the importance of this zone of ours, that because of its lack of shoes [poverty], remains the Achilles' heel of Nicaragua, despite the fact that she could be playing a large part in our development."[9]

He continued to pursue his interest in the more remote regions of Nicaragua. Accompanied by his younger son, Carlos, and his brother-in-law, Carlos Holmann Thompson, he set out for the Coco River, which marks the border between Nicaragua and Honduras. When he returned to Managua he wrote a series of articles for *La Presna* based on his experiences, entitled "Poverty and Hope on Our Sundered Border." (In 1970 he compiled these articles in a book he called *Nuestra Frontera Recortada* or *Our Sundered Border.*)

"Sundered" refers to the fact that Nicaraguans never accepted the arbitration of the Spanish king, Alfonso XIII, when in 1906 he determined that the territory, with its 150-mile coastline on the Caribbean and its 7,000-square-mile area along the Coco River, belonged to Honduras. With no one but Indians in the area and no thought of the resources that might be hidden there, most Nicaraguans were not concerned with what belonged to whom until 1957 when Honduras carved out a new state there and called it "Grácias a Dios" (Thanks Be to God). Suddenly the area became desirable. Tachito sent in a small contingent to reclaim it. Honduras responded with a force of five hundred that promptly scattered the guard. The assignment of that territory to Honduras, as affirmed in a 1960 decision of the International Court of Justice, bothered Pedro Joaquín, who believed its loss contributed to the underdevelopment of the region. He concluded his series of articles with recommendations derived from his experiences traveling from Waspán on the Coco River to Cape Grácias a Dios on the Caribbean. (1) There is a movement of profound significance that is under way in the Coco River region. Nicaraguans should assess it, pay attention to it and support it. (2) That movement has been spurred, especially among the Miskitos, by religious missionaries who have taken them the only hope for a better life. (3) The Miskito has proven to be a competent man who is leaving behind, little by little (for want of the means to leave it more rapidly), the underdeveloped life that he has endured for centuries. (4) The true integration of the coast should begin with the establishment of communication systems between that area and the rest of the country.[10]

The British had created a protectorate in 1655 along the Miskito coast to defend their interests and, ostensibly, the inhabitants from Spanish buccaneers. The Miskitos, led by their own village chiefs, had more autonomy than other indigenous groups. In 1860 the British government acknowledged Nicaragua's sovereignty over the region.[11]

Although Pedro Joaquín was concerned with the well-being of the Miskitos and saw the danger that their continuing isolation posed for Nicaragua, he may not have understood that culturally and linguistically the English-speaking Miskito would be reluctant to be absorbed into the Spanish culture. Many Miskitos still refer to Spanish-speaking Nicaraguans as "los Españoles," or "the Spanish." (The Sandinistas initially made the same error when they undermined the Miskito tradition of autonomy in the early 1980s. Their early misperceptions and resulting abuses, including forced relocation of entire villages, made it easier for contra forces to use the Miskitos to cultivate Indian resistance to the Sandinistas.)

Refreshed from his travels, Pedro Joaquín returned to the offices of *La Prensa*. Rafael Bonilla, general manager of the newspaper, told me in a 1985 interview what it was like to work in those offices:

> The newspaper was like a small republic, and Pedro Joaquín implemented his ideas about society within *La Prensa*. . . .
>
> He instituted fair practices and looked for houses for his workers. There was much freedom in working here. Personnel were like his family; he stimulated them, was very attuned to them. We shared in a percentage of the profits. He began this program on his own—a very rare thing to do. He paid the best salaries. Many people still receive financial assistance from *La Prensa*. When Tomás Borge was imprisoned, his wife received money from *La Prensa*.*

---

*Tomás Borge, Nicaraguan minister of the interior, was imprisoned and

Horacio Ruiz met his future employer in 1946 when Pedro Joaquín had just returned from Mexico with his law degree. In an interview Ruiz described the benefits that Chamorro arranged for his employees.

He considered his earnings to be sufficiently good to share the profits with his workers who had worked 20–25 years and were close to retirement. There had never been Social Security. He gave each retiring worker 10,000 córdobas, which was very significant in that time—about $1,500. With this money they could buy a modest house. His old friends thought he was setting a bad example. They feared their workers would want the same treatment. He eventually worked out a system whereby 10 percent of the profits would be distributed to the workers in accordance with their seniority and positions.

One of the happiest moments for him was when the Social Security law was about to be passed. Even though he was always in opposition to Somoza, on that day he admitted that the dictator had done a good thing. He then assumed part of the worker's contribution to Social Security so the burden on the employee would not be so great.

When someone got sick, or Social Security didn't cover that person's needs, Pedro Joaquín always helped. This attitude still persists. For example, if a worker needs eyeglasses, or has an illness requiring expensive care, *La Prensa* is there to help.

Edgar Castillo, international editor, remembered a personal experience that showed that Pedro Joaquín's generosity was tempered by good sense: "Upon arriving at work one morning, there was a young man who asked for help because he couldn't afford to buy a coffin for a deceased family member. When Pedro Joaquín heard the story, he gave me the money to give to the youth, but then suggested that I ac-

---

tortured after Somoza García's assassination. The only remaining founder of the Frente Sandinista who is still living, he was in prison at the beginning of the 1979 revolution. He and other political prisoners were exchanged for congressmen the Sandinistas had taken hostage. Upon his release he learned that his wife had been taken to a National Guard outpost where she had been raped, tortured, and killed.

company him to see if the coffin were really needed. When I got to the barrio where the young man lived, I learned from his mother that the deceased had already been buried. The boy then confessed to making up the story to get money from *La Prensa*. Pedro Joaquín was very bothered by this. He hated to be lied to."

Dr. Emilio Álvarez Montalván was not a member of the *La Prensa* family but was a loving friend of the Chamorros. In Pedro Joaquín's study, the doctor told me about his friend's relationship to his employees and the newspaper: "All employees at *La Prensa* were treated like family. Pedro Joaquín was very proud to be 'paterfamilias.' He wanted to be kind to his employees, not pressuring them too much, but at the same time he wanted the paper to be a success." Álvarez Montalván pointed out that although Pedro Joaquín could be kind and giving, he could also be very demanding: "If *La Prensa* were closed by Somoza, it was a failure. He had to keep it alive and also the best. He asked for excellence and was always teaching about excellence. He was a great success as an administrator with his technical knowledge and organizational ability. But he was irascible over simple things and so lived with great tension."

Edgar Castillo's review of a typical morning at *La Prensa* reveals Chamorro's administrative style: "When Pedro Joaquín arrived at 8:15 every morning, he would first ask, 'Who wrote this article?' And he would congratulate the writer if he liked it. But if he didn't like one, he would call the writer into his office and talk to him. He would check on the thoroughness of the reporting that went into the article. He wanted everything to be carefully verified. He would frequently talk with the heads of the departments, asking each how his department was going. If a photo turned out poorly, he would inquire as to the paper or ink. The next day the photos would be better. He would check on circulation and ask those in charge why circulation was low here or there. He would speak with each department head and then went to his office to write his editorials."

In addition to his sense of fair play, his concern for his employees' working and social conditions, and his efficiency as an administrator, Pedro Joaquín possessed qualities of character that brought strength to the newspaper and inspired pride in his staff. Horacio Ruiz attested to these qualities:

The paper was suffering before Pedro Joaquín took over. He brought in another mentality—dynamic, informed; it became an instrument of social justice. He was firm, disciplined, and determined, with a profound sense of justice. He had an awareness of his own background, but could easily meet humble people—all of which surprised and shocked the wealthier classes, where firm social lines are drawn.

Little by little many of Pedro Joaquín's friends left him because of commercial deals they had made with Tachito Somoza. For Pedro Joaquín, everything connected with Somoza was unacceptable. One time he went to a wedding where Somoza was also in attendance. Somoza was the first to arrive and Pedro Joaquín, the second. Both sat at opposite ends of the reception hall. Somoza sent a messenger to Pedro Joaquín, asking him to join him, but Pedro Joaquín would not.

He was a powerful political leader, but instead of putting his own name forth, he would help others. Many of those he helped later showed their true colors in their alliances with Somoza. He felt badly seeing his friends fall by the wayside.

He pushed the country ahead during the dictatorship. People would become resigned, but he forced them to be aware. There was a spirit of sacrifice about him. He had been a prisoner for so long—during his best years. It is hard for others who have not had these experiences to understand.

Once he went to a meeting of a directorship of the Conservative party that was held in a certain neighborhood. Someone asked him if he would head the group. He would not accept unless he had been elected by all the party members in the barrio. The directors couldn't understand why they should have elections knowing that Pedro Joaquín would be elected. He insisted that the vote take place. He had an obsession—perhaps exaggerated—about democracy. He believed he was doing God's will, fighting His crusade, and that he would not be killed.

In 1977 the Sandinista insurrection was beginning. Pedro Joaquín wanted everyone to participate. (Remember that he defended Sandino as a nationalist and not a Communist. He tried to clean up the image of Sandino during the Somoza years.)

In the Service of Truth and Justice

Chamorro published his essay on Sandino in an April 1967 issue of *La Prensa*. This essay was reprinted on January 10, 1981, in honor of the third anniversary of Pedro Joaquín's death and as a reminder to those who had forgotten Sandino's anti-Communist position:

> Say what you will about him, Sandino is the greatest modern day hero of our country, and his memory should be safeguarded with affection in the hearts of all Nicaraguans.
>
> Sandino represents the rebellion of a people, and his glorious feats in the Segovias Mountains have brought recognition and prestige to Nicaragua from all over the world.
>
> It is certain that during the war he conducted, Sandino made mistakes and committed injustices. Likewise, the interventionists made mistakes and committed injustices and crimes.
>
> It is not true that Sandino was a Communist, but he was a nationalist, which is different. . . .
>
> The Communists used to say that the idea of "country" was a middle-class complex, and they continue to think the same even though they don't admit it because the political interests of Russia and the diffusion of its doctrine are more important to them than "country."
>
> Sandino was not able to accept the internationalization that the Communists pursue because he essentially was a nationalist and a patriot, that is, the opposite of what fundamentally the Communists are.
>
> The figure of Sandino must be extolled precisely in order to oppose the Communists who obey the interventionist collaborators of Russia and China.
>
> Sandino fought against the United States Marines, but he did not bring Russian Cossacks to Nicaragua as did Fidel Castro in Cuba.
>
> There is a vast difference between the Communist, Fidel Castro, who in his unfaithful fight for independence of his country, filled it with rockets, soldiers, planes and even Russian canned goods, and Sandino, who defended the sovereignty of his country with homemade bombs rather than accept the intervention of another country.

Sandino was great because he was not led to Communist treason like Castro, but rather was motivated by an Indo-Hispanic ideal.

Naturally, the Communists, who attacked and slandered Sandino when he was in the mountains, now try to use his name because they do not have any moral obstacle stopping them from using whatever thing serves their purposes or brings prestige to their propaganda.

Sandino was a pure product of our land, very different from those Russian or Chinese exports, and, as such, we must elevate his figure and keep his memory in mind.

His valorous actions were Nicaraguan, not Soviet, and his nationalism was indigenous, not Russian.

Sandino is a monument to the dignity of our country, and we must not permit the Communists, with whom he never cooperated, to dirty his memory by using the honor of his figure as a pretext for combatting imperialism while delivering our land to Russia as Castro delivered Cuba.[12]

In his crusade, Pedro Joaquín was not beyond using embarrassment and humor as a device to criticize the Somozas and their supporters, according to editor Carlos Ramírez: "Pedro Joaquín had a visitor who was, at the time, presiding over the Nicaraguan Congress. *La Prensa* had published a photo of the gentleman bending to pick up a medal which Somoza had dropped on the floor. The photo gave the impression of a very servile man groveling at Somoza's feet. The official was so enraged that he stalked into *La Prensa* with a gun, threatening to kill Pedro Joaquín, who calmly talked him out of it."

Chamorro's criticism was not confined to Nicaraguans who supported Somoza. Dr. Álvarez Montalván explained that Pedro Joaquín's ideals caused him to criticize the United States for its support of the dictatorship. "In the United States," said the doctor, "Pedro Joaquín was respected but not liked." The doctor described his friend as being "a dictator in his own way" (a thought later expressed by Claudia, Chamorro's elder daughter). He also brought out other dimensions of Pedro Joaquín's personality:

He liked to drink because it made him easygoing. He especially enjoyed the "tertulia" where he could get together with friends or political and business associates. The "tertulia," or regular gathering of a circle of friends, usually men, is an old Spanish tradition and provides an informal way to reach business agreements.

But he became very brash and sometimes furious with his friends when he drank. But the next day he always asked the pardon of those he offended. He had a charming sweetness about him. He never told dirty stories or engaged in mud-slinging. He never offended anyone by using their private lives against them.

Pedro Joaquín had a simple sense of humor. He loved playing jokes on his friends, like hiding a *Playboy* magazine in a suitcase of a friend so that his wife would find it.

In his youth, he had a great admiration for bullfighters and especially admired Manolete. He even had one of his capes. Pedro Joaquín broke a rib bullfighting once. He had to live life with the highest of tension.

The tension Pedro Joaquín lived with reached pinnacle proportions on December 23, 1972, at 12:30 A.M. An earthquake that measured 6.3 on the Richter scale killed 10,000 people and left 300,000 homeless in a city of 400,000. Three-fourths of Managua's buildings had been leveled or damaged beyond repair.

In his short novel, *Richter 7,* published in 1976, Chamorro described the terror, confusion, and sorrow of the people. In the introduction he wrote that at first people responded with great concern toward one another. "Never had there been so much brotherhood in the world." There was a cohesiveness, an awareness that "this time man had not been the perpetrator of the catastrophe."[13] As people started to assess their losses, however, the spirit of mutual helpfulness, Chamorro's ideal, was replaced by the base behavior that he could not tolerate: "As the sun came out, people began to recognize each other. Each one saw his own disgrace in the image of the other. Differences once again became apparent, and when the sun was high, and the earth no longer trembled, and one could see everything clearly, the peace ended. Then the bitter words were heard; insults began. Envy, rage and self-interest surfaced, and a few hours later the plunder began."[14]

Horacio Ruiz described the scene in an article *La Prensa* published sixty-nine days after the quake: "Christmas charity and the age-old spirit of brotherhood had predominated in the last hours of the condemned city. . . . In that dawn, and in the days that followed, every one of the 400,000 inhabitants of Managua fully tasted death. Thousands never got up. Those who survived will always live with the sensation that something of their own, something alive from each of them, was buried in the city. . . . We experienced what the people from ancient Pompeii had. The ruin, fire, thunder, thirst, hunger, looting and chaos. . . . It will be impossible for future generations to imagine what the people of Managua lived through on December 23, 1972."[15]

The earthquake had destroyed the buildings of *La Prensa* as well as its principal rotary press. With some rescued equipment, including damaged but workable offset presses, *La Prensa* reopened in a newly located building made of sheet metal in March 1973.

What meant death, disease, hunger, and loss for those who lived in the heart of the city, near the epicenter of the quake, turned out to be a fat opportunity for Tachito, who named himself president of the National Emergency Committee. His guard joined in the looting, even using army trucks to haul their booty. Much of the arriving relief found its way to the black market where it brought exorbitant returns. Inflation soared. Food that arrived from the United States within hours of the quake was not distributed for days.

Financial aid that was meant for reconstruction was channeled through Tachito's banks; materials for construction were manufactured in his businesses. What was rebuilt was rebuilt on Somoza's land. Today visitors to Managua, expecting a view of the downtown area from their windows in the Intercontinental Hotel, see only a large, bleak field around which young Sandinista soldiers run to get their daily exercise. Ruins created by the earthquake still stand in downtown Managua. Business owners soon opened new shops in the residential areas where they lived, abandoning central Managua, which was not rebuilt during Tachito's remaining years in office, despite all the foreign financial assistance.

Tachito sold some of his land to the government in order to reap huge returns. This land was to be used as the site of new housing for the refugees. Pedro Joaquín wrote about this transaction:

> Is it possible that while hundreds of children die from dysentery, from the squalor that the earthquake produced, that our society continues to indulge in these archaic, grandiose business arrangements, made at the official level, at the expense of social needs?
>
> They can say that the transactions are legal. They can also justify the price of a square yard and provide their dates of acquisition before the earthquake, but they can never explain the fundamental question: Is it not incredible that after a tragedy like the one of December 23rd, there can be such commerce, such trade, with the lives of the homeless and their children?[16]

No one knows what happened to the U.S. financial aid that arrived in the first six months after the quake but was never accounted for. Bernard Diederich reports that the National Emergency Committee received $24,853,000 in cash. While the United States sent $32 million plus additional funds from private sources, records from the Nicaraguan treasury show that only $16,220,000 had been received.[17]

The businessmen of Managua, who had heretofore put up with Somoza's dictates because of personal favors bestowed on them, became impatient with his behavior following the earthquake. The private-sector growth that had taken place under Tachito's brother Luis had come to a standstill. It seemed that every córdoba was somehow filtered through one of Tachito's business concerns. The businessmen began to organize in opposition. University students, witnessing the government's flagrant corruption, aligned themselves with Marxist-oriented groups. The Frente Sandinista began to recruit among them and gradually grew in influence and strength in the rural areas. Though he failed to realize it, Tachito's greed was seriously undermining his position.

Pedro Joaquín circulated a mimeographed letter to Somoza because censorship prevented its publication. In it he stressed Nicaragua's desperate situation, and in the first paragraph he predicted his own assassination. The letter was reprinted in *La Prensa* on January 10, 1981.

Nicaragua Divided

Señor:

Before bearing your final act of repression, I send you this letter in which I set out certain points about the present situation.

If you could only, General, like that king in the nursery stories, put on a peasant's attire and walk unnoticed through the plazas, or at least send a trustworthy servant to listen to what is being said in the markets, you would know what is really occurring in Nicaragua.

You would know, for example, that members of private enterprises are justifiably fearful because your continuing presence in the government is an attractive pretext for the multiplication of guerrilla groups. These businessmen are also tired of enduring your constant advances into areas which traditionally have been the economic concerns of large and small businesses while you are sheltered by public power. They are not going to complain directly to you because they know they would be risking too much.

You would also know—and without having to disguise yourself as a peasant—the sentiments of the workers and peasants toward your regime. They, like the majority of our citizens, including enlightened members of your own party, privately discuss the guerrilla situation, observing that if you continue in power, the situation will worsen. Your long regime has been an extraordinary force behind the proliferation of guerrilla activities.

I am not involved in any way in these activities although you arbitrarily insist upon linking me with them. This type of thinking further polarizes the already combative politics of the country and carries them, to your discredit, to the point where from here on there will be armed Somocistas and armed Sandinistas.

Try to see the truth of this intolerable situation and the urgency of saving the country.[18]

Somoza did not save the country. There would be elections on September 1, 1974, and he would "run against" Edmundo Paguaga Irías who, while calling himself a Conservative candidate, was in fact one of Somoza's supporters. A group of concerned citizens, including lawyers, laborers, and opposition party leaders, formally protested the elections. Representing political viewpoints from far left to far right, they called themselves "The Twenty-seven." Pedro Joaquín was among the group that pressed for an election boycott. To him the boycott made sense, since there was no one to vote for.

Tachito took the group to court and charged them with "inciting to abstain"—an illegal activity. They were found guilty and their "civil liberties" were suspended. None would be allowed to travel.

Strikes followed. Chamorro was threatened with arrest, as was any journalist who defamed government officials. The day before the election Pedro Joaquín ran the headline "Candidates Who Won Tomorrow's Elections."[19] As predicted, Somoza won. Diederich described the elections: "Although 40 percent of the electorate did abstain, Tacho's vote counters declared that he had received 748,985 of the 815,758 votes cast. There was no secret ballot. When a ballot was marked, the mark could be clearly seen through the thin paper. It was imperative for almost everyone to be recorded as having voted 'Nationalist Liberal,' because only those who voted for Somoza were given the ID card called a 'magnífica,' required for all government employees."[20]

The government proclaimed that 70 percent of the 1,150,000 registered voters had cast ballots. A U.S. embassy official, quoted by Diederich, said, "It's hard to believe that in a country of two million, that many were inscribed." Children were also allowed to vote, and they were seen showing off their red-inked fingers, a sign to all that they had voted.[21]

On December 27, 1974, a wealthy businessman, José María Castillo Quant, and his prominent guests, including Tachito's brother-in-law, were taken hostage by a group of men and women belonging to the Frente Sandinista. They demanded the release of political prisoners, $5 million to fund their cause, an increase in the minimum wage for Nicaraguan workers, publication of the Frente's rationale and purposes to be communicated in all the media, freedom of information, and cessation of all repressive measures. The release of the prisoners, deliverance of the money, and proof that the other demands had been met were to be demonstrated within thirty-six hours. Archbishop Miguel Obando y Bravo was the liaison between the Sandinistas and Somoza.

Tachito was outraged. To concede to the demands would be the ultimate humiliation. Yet his brother-in-law was among the hostages,

59

as were many of his powerful supporters. Some compromises were made, but the victory belonged to the Sandinistas. Somoza abuses were broadcast; $1 million, rather than $5 million, was paid; the prisoners, including the current president of Nicaragua, Daniel Ortega, were released.

The hostages, with the exception of Castillo Quant, who was killed picking up a gun, accompanied the Sandinistas and the rescued political prisoners to the airport where they departed for Cuba. Throngs cheered their passing. It was a turning point for the Sandinista movement and its leaders, who were now considered heroes. In less than five years, with the support of the majority of Nicaraguans, the Sandinistas would celebrate the triumph of the revolution.

The Sandinistas' effrontery prompted Tachito to unleash his guard. In an August 1977 report, Amnesty International described the repression that took place during this period of martial law: "The unprotected rural population bears the brunt of abuses of human rights incurred as a result of counterinsurgency operations. . . . Local leaders reportedly are tortured and murdered as a routine method to uncover FSLN guerrillas and to discourage local support."[22]

Tachito wanted retribution, and he extracted much of it from Pedro Joaquín by ordering him to publish, on three consecutive days, an accusation that held Chamorro and *La Prensa* responsible for "trying to create an atmosphere of hatred so that, when the time was ripe, it could place the government in a shameful position." Tachito would have liked to take Pedro Joaquín to court under a new article of the penal code he had just enacted: "If it is not possible to find out who committed an act of terrorism, its promoters or instigators will be held responsible for it."[23]

Forbidden from publishing a rebuttal, Chamorro responded to Tachito with another mimeographed letter that said: "The regrettable deaths and injuries caused by the raid on Dr. José María Castillo's house are not the fruits of my harvest, but of the violence your regime has institutionalized for many years."[24]

Tachito could not throw Pedro Joaquín in prison again because he had become too influential an adversary, too well known among the press corps and, in particular, among the members of the Inter-

Pedro Joaquín sailing on Lake Nicaragua (from La Patria de Pedro*).*

At home in Managua. Left to right: top row, *Pedro Joaquín, Dona Margarita Cardenal de Chamorro (Pedro Joaquín's mother), Ana Maria Chamorro Cardenal (de Holmann), Ligia Chamorro Cardenal (de Barreto);* seated, middle row, *Dr. Pedro Joaquín Chamorro Zelaya (Pedro Joaquín's father) with two bishops;* bottom row, *Xavier and Jaime Chamorro Cardenal (from* La Patria de Pedro*).*

In the mountains of Chontales, June 1959; Pedro Joaquín at bottom left (from La Patria de Pedro).

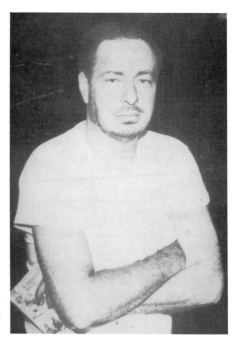

Pedro Joaquín awaiting sentencing, 1959 (from La Patria de Pedro).

The Chamorros in Costa Rica, 1959 (from La Patria de Pedro*).*

Pedro Joaquín in his office at La Prensa, *1963 (from* La Patria de Pedro).

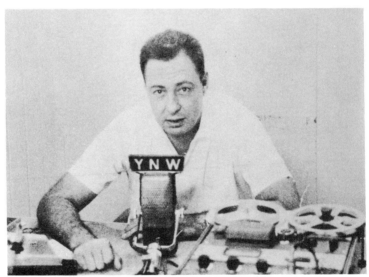

Pedro Joaquín in 1967 broadcasting "A Media Journada: 5 P.M." (in Spanish news jargon, "Halfway through the day's printing") (from La Patria de Pedro).

On their patio, left to right: *Violeta, Cristiana, Pedro Joaquín, Claudia (from* La Patria de Pedro*).*

Chamorro family (Violeta in center) in procession accompanying body of Pedro Joaquín (from La Prensa Cincuentenario*).*

"Here fell Pedro J. Chamorro C.,"
marker with wreaths (from La Prensa
Cincuentenario*).*

Mourners offering condolences to Car-
los Fernandez and Cristiana (from La
Prensa Cincuentenario*).*

Violeta and Dr. Emilio Álvarez Montalván in Pedro Joaquín's study (photo by author).

Violeta at her husband's grave (photo by author).

Pedro Joaquín's study (photo by author).

*Dr. Emilio Álvarez Montalván stands beside the car that
Pedro Joaquín was driving when he was shot and killed
(photo by author).*

FSLN grafitti on the monument to Pedro Joaquín (photo by author).

American Press Association. But Tachito did not forget the mimeographed letters: "We have introduced censorship, and on more than twenty occasions he, Pedro Joaquín, has sent clandestine letters to his subscribers, always in the hope that the authorities would take reprisals against him, so that he could play the role of victim. After careful consideration, we arrived at the conclusion that those letters would not, let us say, provoke a demonstration on the streets. So we have let him be. But we have it all in his record! He has broken the law, and we are keeping it all in his record until this insubordination is translated into action. And when that happens, he will have to face our justice."[25]

Even though his pen was restrained by censorship, Pedro Joaquín would not be outmaneuvered. In 1974 he brought together all of the opposition—the dissident Liberals, Conservatives, Christian Socialists, intellectuals, and labor leaders—under the banner of the Democratic Union of Liberation (UDEL). As its elected president, Pedro Joaquín organized meetings in both rural and urban areas. He got to know intimately the problems of the peasants and wrote a book in their honor, *Jesús Marchena,* about a humble man from Rivas, in southwestern Nicaragua.[26] (According to Ohio University professors Grafton Conliffe and Thomas Walker in a 1978 issue of *Caribbean Review,* Jesús became "a symbol of all Nicaraguans tortured and crucified by an insensitive government.")[27]

Eduardo Crawley interviewed Pedro Joaquín when he was in the midst of organizing UDEL. Long labeled a Conservative he was aware of the stain on the Chamorro name from his ancestor Emiliano Chamorro's part in the 1916 Bryan-Chamorro treaty. The treaty granted the United States all rights to a trans-Nicaraguan canal that would join the Caribbean with the Pacific and permitted a U.S. naval base in the Gulf of Fonseca—all for $3 million. The treaty, which disregarded a previous border agreement with Costa Rica and did not have the backing of the Nicaraguan people, was not recognized by other Central American countries because it ignored their concerns and was the product of U.S. intervention.[28]

Trappist priest Ernesto Cardinal, Nicaragua's minister of culture, wrote a 1981 essay for the pro-Sandinista newspaper, *Nuevo Amanecer Cultural (New Cultural Dawn),* in which he described his cousin Pedro

Joaquín's political background and attitude toward being labeled a Conservative. He minced no words in claiming him to be a hero of the revolution:

> Pedro Joaquín was never a Conservative. Those who knew him as intimately as I know that very well. Those who pay him homage as a Conservative betray him, falsifying his image. . . . Pedro Joaquín launched violent attacks against Conservatives and Liberals as seen in the old collections of *La Prensa*. . . .
>
> Even though he was a Chamorro, he presented himself as anti-Chamorro. Chamorrismo was principally represented by Emiliano who had signed pacts with Somoza. . . .
>
> After the failure of Olama and Mollejones [the April rebellion of 1959], Pedro Joaquín decided to declare himself a Conservative, but for tactical reasons. He needed a platform from which to continue fighting against the dictatorship. Many times he told me of the shame he felt having to call himself "Conservative." . . .
>
> It is clear to me that he did not have personal ambition, and that his obsession was the fall of Somoza. He dreamed about the new Nicaragua that would emerge. I remember, about 1960, when I had left the monastery, that he talked to me about the changes there would be in the country. And they were things that the Sandinista revolution has realized. He also wanted other, more extreme things, that this revolution has not done.
>
> The reactionaries do not have the right to use Pedro Joaquín's name. This is not to say that Pedro would turn over in his grave, but he has left the tomb, and he is with the people. Pedro Joaquín belongs to the revolution. He has been, from the day of his death, property of the people.[29]

Pedro Joaquín disassociated himself from his ancestor's politics in the interview with Crawley: "Somoza likes to cast me in the role of the reactionary, right-wing Conservative who is battling for the restoration of lost privileges, but I have never been a Conservative in the strict sense of the word. The problem is that in Nicaragua the name Chamorro and the title 'Conservative' have almost become synonymous. But it makes no sense to be a Conservative in this day and age."[30] He saw himself as a "Social Christian"—a very vulnerable one: "It is an easy matter for anyone to kill me," he stated. "I have no bodyguards, and I drive around alone and unarmed."[31]

Although Pedro Joaquín took no special precautions to safeguard his life, a watchful group of journalists from the Inter-American Press Association did. Chamorro had been president of the association from 1953 to 1959 and had used its conferences since then as a forum from which to lambast the Somozas. The IAPA had sent intermediaries in 1954 and 1956 when Pedro Joaquín had been implicated in the plots to kill Somoza García. After his escape to Costa Rica in 1957, the IAPA requested that he be granted asylum by the Costa Rican president, José Figueres.[32]

Pedro Joaquín and the representative from Tachito's newspaper, *Novedades (Latest News),* attended the 1977 IAPA conference in Santo Domingo, Dominican Republic. Chamorro's accusations of unwarranted press censorship and human rights abuses were denied by his competitor in an interview published in the Dominican newspaper *Listín Diario (Daily News).* Chamorro, nevertheless, had the last word:

> Somoza's representative told *Listín Diario* that I am going to end up like Miguel Ángel Quevedo, who was said to have committed suicide. Why say such a thing about a person without any apparent economic or family problems? It isn't the first time that they tell me this because it is a way of threatening my life. It is like telling me, "we are going to kill you, and there will be no assassin's sign." This is the same thing they have done with so many people in Nicaragua. To cite only one case, just a few weeks ago the engineer, Raul Gonzales, was cudgeled to death in the prison in Estelí, and later there was an official announcement affirming that he had died in a fight with the Army.
>
> Somoza's agent sounds like a broken record saying that everything that happens in Nicaragua against him is the work of Fidel Castro. Today, the Dominican newspapers published a Managuan cable in which the Somoza government accuses a group of conspiracy. This group includes a millionaire owner of the principal chain of supermarkets, an owner of an instant coffee factory, several intellectuals, poets, novelists and three priests.
>
> How can this contradiction be explained? Is it possible that

this conspiracy of millionaires and priests is directed by Fidel Castro? What is happening is simply that the Nicaraguan people—all the people, rich and poor—have had enough of the Somoza tyranny.[33]

In addition to his journalistic protests, Pedro Joaquín continued to protest by writing fiction during the years before his death. Besides *Jesús Marchena,* written in 1975, and *Richter 7*, in 1976, he wrote a collection of short stories entitled *El enigma de las alemanas (The Enigma of the German Girls)*. This book won first prize in a Central American literature contest sponsored by the Guatemalan Institute of Hispanic Culture. Conliffe and Walker describe Chamorro's writings and his character in their 1978 article: "Pedro Joaquín Chamorro was an intelligent and concerned writer capable of producing a novel of ideas as well as creative fiction. At the same time he was an untiring patriot, a champion of the common man and an advocate of universal love and human dignity. His ghost haunts the decaying Somoza dictatorship and will be present at its downfall."[34]

Censorship and travel restrictions were lifted four months before Pedro Joaquín's death. He was granted permission to travel to New York City and Columbia University in November 1977 to receive the Maria Moors Cabot Prize given in recognition of "distinguished journalistic contributions to the advancement of inter-American understanding." The award was made by William G. McGill, then president of Columbia. Testimony included the following notes on Pedro Joaquín's life: "Although he is 53 years old, Pedro Chamorro has never voted in a Nicaraguan election. Since he attained voting age, the editor of *La Prensa* has found himself in jail or in exile during all but one election. On that occasion, in 1972, he organized a boycott of the electoral process and was again arrested."[35]

Four days before his death, Pedro Joaquín wrote an editorial in response to the burgeoning of radical rhetoric heard in Managua. He was dedicated to the ideal of a revolution that would result in a democracy. His words in the editorial "Palabrería y burguesía" (Hollow Speech and the Bourgeoisie) reflected his impatience with those who would claim the revolution for themselves. The editorial was reprinted in *La Prensa* on January 10, 1981, as a protest against the Sandinistas.

In the Service of Truth and Justice

An enormous percent of the Nicaraguan people belong to the bourgeoisie—high, middle or low, like those who have grocery stores, the artisans, the manufacturers of small items . . . the middle-class farmer and even the peasant whom we could refer to as the rural bourgeoisie, with his colt, cow, coffee, cane, bean or corn crops, sold in the towns and cities. These are bourgeoisie and not proletariats.

Sure the majority of our population is made up of peasants and workers, but the low and middle classes, people who earn their living with the sweat of their brows, and whose support of national production is considerable, should not be marginalized, and much less deprecated by those who use "proletarian" vocabulary even though their own lives do not in the least resemble that of proletarian life.

We are calling attention to this business because the daily discourses against the "bourgeoisie" have become an integral part of a decaying and demagogic national lexicon. . . . Neither the man who works his parcel of land, nor the woman whose market earnings support all of her family, nor the professional who has studied at the cost of many sacrifices, nor the middle-class landowner, nor the prosperous businessman with progressive ideas are people who should be hated, but worthy persons, part of our people, part of the country and very necessary for its reconstruction.

It is curious and also revealing to observe how that irrational cry against the bourgeoisie does not come from the workers who fight so that their class may be elevated; it doesn't come from union members, but generally has its origin in elements of the bourgeoisie, who want to appear like proletariats.

A true contradiction, don't you think?[36]

There were no contradictions in the powerful tribute given upon Chamorro's death by Pablo Antonio Cuadra, the acting director of *La Prensa,* who had assumed responsibility for the newspaper's publication during Pedro Joaquín's imprisonments and exile. (Once, when an article had been censored, Cuadra published in its place a picture of Ava Gardner. It wasn't long before the people caught on to what all of those photos of Gardner meant. "People continued to buy the newspaper," Cuadra said, "even when there was nothing controversial left to write.")

No photo could transmit Cuadra's thoughts at the sight of Pedro Joaquín's body after his assassination, but his words to me could have spoken for the nation: "I went to the hospital and saw Pedro Joaquín with some thirty shotgun wounds. If he's not a hero, I don't know who is. Pedro's valor was spent for ideals. He was one man alone with a pen in front of a dictator who had the National Guard, prisons and torturers. He stood alone before all of that—one man with a newspaper, a bullfighter without a sword."

CHAPTER 5

REVOLUTION

Outraged by the murder of their leader, members of the Democratic Union of Liberation called for a general strike. Seventy-five percent of industry and business shut down operations, according to the *New York Times*. The offices of *La Prensa* became the hub of strike coordination. Leaders demanded that Somoza resign and that he reveal the "intellectual authors" of Chamorro's assassination. Pablo Antonio Cuadra said that "I see *La Prensa* as the republic of paper fighting the dictatorship of steel."[1]

Tachito refused to resign, saying that he had every intention of staying in office until his term ended in 1981. He invoked a special emergency law to end the strike "with power to impose heavy fines on businesses and industries that defy Government orders to reopen." He also forbade radio and television from broadcasting news of the strike or anything "of an alarming nature or that could cause panic among the citizenry."[2]

Many businessmen, having ignored Somoza abuses when they or their families were not personally affected, were now paying the wages of their striking employees. There would be no dialogue between the leaders of the strike and Tachito, because as Rafael Córdova Rivas, Chamorro's successor as head of the UDEL, told Alan Riding of the *New York Times,* "This is the end of the civil struggle. It's not that we favor violence, but we're no longer interested in talking to Somoza."[3]

The political moderates, who continued to support the strike, wanted President Jimmy Carter to exert pressure on Somoza to step down before events got out of hand. Carter was torn between his human rights ideals and those of nonintervention. At first he criticized Somoza for rights abuses but later sent him a letter that the dictator misinterpreted. The letter, which was meant to encourage progress in the area of human rights, was taken instead as congratulatory—a pat on the back because Tachito had lifted the state of siege he had imposed in response to the strikes and demonstrations. These mixed signals further coalesced the union of the moderate opposition groups with the Sandinistas, who were eager to gain more respectability. What Pedro Joaquín had predicted in his 1975 mimeographed letter to Somoza—that his continuing as president would lead to a strengthening of guerrilla groups—was coming to pass.

Violence broke out on February 21, 1978, in the Indian community of Monimbó, twenty miles southeast of Managua, when National Guardsmen broke up a gathering of people who were attending mass in honor of Pedro Joaquín. The guard used tear gas and rifle butts to disperse the crowd even though the state of siege had been lifted. The townspeople fought back against the tanks and helicopters that were brought in to fortify the guard. After many deaths and an initial defeat, the citizens of Monimbó prevailed. Their courage and tenacity inspired people from other rural communities to engage the guard in hit-and-run forays. The guard now needed heavy air cover to go anywhere in the interior and, according to Bernard Diederich, Monimbó "became the center of anti-Somoza revolt."[4]

On August 22, 1978, twenty-five heavily armed Sandinistas took over the National Palace while Congress was meeting. In return for the 1,500 hostages, they demanded the release of political prisoners, ransom, and safe conduct. Tachito reluctantly met their demands. Again the Nicaraguan people praised the feats of the Sandinistas. The rebels represented their hope for an escape from the dictatorship.*

---

*In August 1978 the Chamorro family loaned the Sandinistas $50,000 for a "revolutionary operation." They now believe it to have been the National Palace takeover, led by Eden Pastora. The debt has not yet been repaid. See Jaime Chamorro, *La Prensa: The Republic of Paper* (New York: Freedom House, 1989), 11. Pedro Joaquín Chamorro Barrios (Quinto) told me in an August 5, 1989, telephone interview that the loan represented half

Revolution

The capture of the palace and the congressmen represented an enormous humiliation for the Somoza regime. To show that he still had control over Nicaragua, Tachito used his guard and their powerful military machinery to subdue the Sandinista outposts one by one. While Tachito was trying to purge the country of Sandinistas, the population engaged in another general strike—a nonviolent means of protest that reflected the people's unhappiness and disillusionment with him.

In the meantime Venezuelan president Carlos Andrés Pérez led the international political debate over Somoza's betrayal of democratic principles. He urged the OAS to sponsor mediation to bring about an end to the conflict. The United States chose to step softly because of its noninterventionist position. (It is ironic that after having formally intervened since 1909 in the affairs of Nicaragua—an intervention that led to the forty-two-year-long Somoza regime—the United States resisted pressures that might have made amends for the past.)

In September 1978 the Sandinistas encouraged citizens to rise in a nationwide rebellion against the National Guard and gave them arms with which to do it. The citizens, supportive of their boys—"los muchachos"—helped the Sandinistas take control of the outlying cities. Somoza likened his all-out defense to the American experience in Vietnam, calling it another "Tet Offensive."[5] In massive reply to their challenge, he killed civilians and Sandinistas alike. Summary executions were commonplace. Youths were frequently rounded up from poor barrios, lined up, and shot as a means to eradicate Sandinista reinforcements.

Meanwhile mediation was delayed because Tachito wanted representatives from Guatemala and El Salvador to participate, as both countries were governed by military dictators sympathetic to him. However, he refused to agree on Colombia's participation because it had joined with Venezuela in condemning him before the United Nations, charging that he was responsible for a "wave of genocide."[6] Eventually it was decided that the United States, the Dominican Republic, and Guatemala would send mediators to Nicaragua.

William Bowdler, the seasoned U.S. delegate, admitted after long,

---

of the $100,000 *La Prensa* had received from longtime friend Carlos Andrés Pérez, president of Venezuela.

agonizing efforts that there was no chance for a peaceful settlement as long as Somoza remained in office. He finally came right out and asked the dictator to resign. Tachito responded firmly that he had no intention of leaving office. Eager to get something settled, the foreign mediators urged a plebiscite in which the people would decide whether they wanted Somoza to stay. Mediation members representing the opposition coalition were adamant in their assertion that there could be no plebiscite unless the guard was absent from the scene.

Graham Greene, the British novelist, explains the Nicaraguans' mistrust of elections in his book about Omar Torrijos of Panama, *Getting to Know the General:* "During his long reign, Somoza had frequently called elections and, thus, had legitimized his dictatorship, if only in the eyes of the United States, by winning all of them with huge majorities. So 'election' for most people in the crowd was a word which meant trickery. 'No election' was a promise to them of no trickery."[7]

In the United States some congressmen were urging President Carter and Congress to take prompt military action to help Somoza stave off a "Communist takeover" in Nicaragua. Gradually the representatives of the Nicaraguan opposition perceived that what the foreign negotiators really wanted was "Somocismo" without Somoza—the same governmental structure, its priorities and values, and the National Guard. But in the minds of the Nicaraguans, there could be no place for the guard in the new Nicaragua.

The Sandinistas, not wanting any remnant of the previous government, increased their pressure against it. Because of Somoza's bomb attacks, people in the war zones fled to Managua, where food was scarce. Harvests failed. Although the United States had stopped sending military assistance to Somoza, he was able to procure arms from Israel, El Salvador, Guatemala, Brazil, and Argentina to help maintain his position. In an attempt to balance the fight, Carlos Andrés Pérez of Venezuela and Omar Torrijos of Panama gave military assistance to the Sandinistas.[8]

On January 10, 1979, the first anniversary of Pedro Joaquín's death, ten thousand people marched to his grave to place flowers, wreaths, and the black and red Sandinista flag. Somoza's guard dispersed the crowds with shots and tear gas as they left the cemetery.

Revolution

On June 11, 1979, Tachito struck a final blow against *La Prensa* when he ordered the National Guard to destroy it. On that afternoon an armored vehicle fired directly on the building. Guards then scaled the fence and poured gasoline over the structure as terrified employees escaped through the rear. A Cessna flew overhead and launched rockets at what remained of the newspaper office. (The newspaper reopened in the city of León in August, using a rented press. In 1980 it returned to Managua, using a West German loan and equipment donated by the Inter-American Press Association.)[9]

The United States, still reluctant to intervene in a heavy-handed way, resorted to political pressure and removed half of its diplomatic force and its Peace Corps volunteers. The guard was not troubled by U.S. censure and continued its practices of kidnapping, torture, and execution. *La Prensa* published daily the gory details surrounding the disappearances.

Fernando Cardenal, a former Jesuit priest now the minister of education, said that Carter "was betting on a sick horse. Iran should serve as an example."[10] Adolfo Calero-Portocarrero, general manager of the largest soft-drink bottling company in Nicaragua, said that he was not like those who blamed the United States for everything, but he did hold the nation partly responsible: "They did not use their goodwill to help. I don't see the U.S. doing a damn thing. . . . It took thousands of lives even to begin the implementation of the human rights program and for the United States to come out with firm action—sanctions."[11] (Calero, imprisoned for his role during the general strike, became a major political leader of the contras in January 1983.)

The battle finally came to Managua in the early months of 1979. As they did in outlying cities, women and children helped to build barricades and acted as couriers. Tachito's air force strafed them along with the Sandinistas, as they had done elsewhere. People were homeless, hungry, and in need of medical attention. Health conditions worsened with the growing number of corpses that could not be retrieved and buried. Mothers searched daily for their "disappeared" sons at the site near Lake Managua that was used to dispose of those who had been executed, hands tied behind their backs.

Somoza's military strength began to erode because the United

States would no longer help him, despite his entreaty that he was fighting an international Communist conspiracy. The cold-blooded murder of ABC correspondent Bill Stewart by a National Guardsman did not help Tachito's cause. On the evening of June 20, 1979, horrified TV viewers in the United States watched replays of Stewart's execution. He was shot in the head after having first been brutally kicked when he followed orders to lie on the ground. The guards also killed his Nicaraguan interpreter. Members of the news team who remained in the car filming the event barely escaped with their lives. Their survival was due to clever lies told by their Nicaraguan driver, who assured the guards that the team represented Somoza's Channel Six and who promised that the witnesses would claim Stewart had been killed by Sandinista snipers.[12]

One week after the correspondent's death, Lawrence Pezullo was sent as the new U.S. ambassador to Nicaragua to increase the pressure on Somoza to resign, while trying to ensure that some of his supporters would still exert their influence on the newly formed junta that the opposition coalition had just accepted. The junta members and their constituents, however, refused to allow Somocista participation. Named to the junta were Pedro Joaquín's widow, Violeta, Alfonso Robelo, Daniel Ortega, Sergio Ramírez, and Moises Hassan Morales. The two non-Sandinista members, Violeta de Chamorro and Alfonso Robelo, left the junta in 1980. Although Violeta ostensibly left for health reasons, she admitted to serious political and ideological differences with other junta members. On November 4, 1984, Daniel Ortega was elected president of Nicaragua and Sergio Ramírez vice president. Alfonso Robelo became a leader of the contras.

Beaten militarily and psychologically, Tachito finally agreed to go. The United States continued to press for the inclusion of Somocistas on the junta and for the continuing presence of the National Guard. In regard to U.S. policies, junta member Robelo said that there was "no reason why the United States should lay down conditions on how we should run Nicaragua. We see no logic to broadening the junta. . . . After all, it had the support of Nicaragua's largest moderate opposition political and business groups. We're fighting to eliminate Somoza— and they're trying to maintain parts of the National Guard."[13]

Revolution

Managua Archbishop, now Cardinal, Miguel Obando y Bravo likewise criticized the United States: "We are thankful for the understanding and collaboration of those governments who have shown interest in our people's situation but at the same time we lament the ambiguity of those governments who have thought or continue to think of their own political interests before the common good of the Nicaraguan people."[14]

Somoza resigned the presidency on July 16, 1979, and fled to Florida. His temporary successor, Francisco Urcuyo, who had been entrusted with turning over the reins of government to the new junta, balked when it was time for the change, even though the guard was now a shambles, many members clamoring to escape or trying to conceal themselves as ordinary citizens. Tachito had to call from Florida, saying that the United States would not let him stay if Urcuyo did not step down. Urcuyo left for Guatemala, and the first Junta of National Reconstruction, which already was recognized by nine countries, came to power. Diederich summarizes what Nicaraguans refer to as "the triumph": "Guided by a comparatively small group of guerrillas within months after the death of Pedro Joaquín Chamorro, an event that acted as a catalyst, all sectors of Nicaraguan society were in some way involved in the movement to oust Somoza and the end of the dynastic dictatorship."[15]

Chamorro had believed that only a few Sandinistas were Marxists and that their influence would diminish with Somoza's departure. In a *New York Times* interview two months before his death, Pedro Joaquín said that "without Somoza there would never be a Frente Sandinista. Just as without Batista there would never be a Fidel Castro in Cuba."[16]

In a 1979 article in *Foreign Affairs,* William LeoGrande, a professor at the American University, analyzed the fumbling reactions of the United States to the transition of power in Nicaragua: "As events unfolded in Nicaragua, the U.S. consistently tried to fit a square peg of policy into the round hole of reality. By failing to assess accurately the dynamics of Somoza's decline, the U.S. produced proposals which were invariably six months out of date. When the political initiative lay with the moderate opposition, the U.S. acted as if it still lay with

Somoza. When the initiative shifted to the radicals, the U.S. acted as if it lay with the moderates. And when, at the last moment, the U.S. recognized that the radicals held the initiative, it seemed to think it could cajole them into returning it to the moderates."[17]

CHAPTER 6

FAMILY LEGACY

After his brother's death, Xavier Chamorro became codirector of *La Prensa*, assisted by Pablo Antonio Cuadra and Danilo Aguirre Solís. Aguirre was president of the Union of Nicaraguan Journalists, a Sandinista organization that dealt with the certification of journalists. Xavier wanted the newspaper to give editorial support to the aims of the Sandinista revolution, and Aguirre encouraged this move. Many articles reflected that orientation. A contravening force, however, came from Pedro Joaquín's son Quinto, who said that he had been suspicious of the Sandinistas from the beginning. Quinto may have been exposed to Communist rhetoric from people his own age who had joined the Sandinistas. He may also have remembered his father's fear that the continuation of the Somoza regime could lead to a domination of Communist ideology in the revolution. Now with the moderating voice of his father stilled, Quinto's suspicions mounted that the Sandinistas would influence inordinately the course of the revolution. His articles often stood in square opposition to Sandinista methods and programs. Because of this ideological struggle, there was little editorial consistency at the newspaper.

Xavier, mild-tempered and loved by *La Prensa*'s staff, offered his resignation to the Chamorro board of directors, but they were not ready to accept it. The Sandinista leadership wanted him to hold on to his position for a while so that Violeta's resignation from the junta and his departure from *La Prensa* would not be a media coup for their critics.

75

Nicaragua Divided

The newspaper staff knew that if Xavier resigned, their new leader would be Quinto, who was already sales manager and a member of both the editorial board and the board of directors. They thought, however, that Quinto lacked the delicacy and grace of both his father and his uncle. They may have wanted to express freely the revolutionary fervor that was spreading throughout the country without having to worry about Quinto's mitigating voice. After all, had not Pedro Joaquín demonstrated affection for the Sandinistas? Had he not dedicated his adult life to fighting the Somoza dynasty? If he were still alive, would he not have been in the forefront of these last stages before Somoza's overthrow? It must have seemed to most of the *La Prensa* staff that Xavier, not Quinto, was in step with Pedro Joaquín's ideals and goals. With the tension worsening between the two political camps, and the resulting lack of cohesion and security among the workers, the board of directors accepted Xavier's resignation in July 1980, giving him 25 percent of *La Prensa's* capital to begin *El Nuevo Diario (The New Daily)*. News director Danilo Aguirre Solís and 70 percent of the employees accompanied Xavier, most of them, according to Jaime Chamorro, "technical" staff. Sixty percent of the editors, 70 percent of the managers, and 40 percent of the "primary" staff stayed at *La Prensa*.[1]

In an August 5, 1989, telephone interview Quinto explained that the remaining staff signed a petition, addressed to the board of directors, that he be named codirector with Pablo Antonio Cuadra. Their wish was granted. With Xavier's departure to *El Nuevo Diario,* and with his twenty-eight-year-old nephew installed at *La Prensa,* the ideological positions represented by these men and those who supported them were made manifest in both newspapers.

In 1984 Sandinista censorship tightened around *La Prensa* in response to what the junta called a state of war caused by U.S. aggression, in the form of a surrogate army called the contras. Quinto made his political statement by leaving Nicaragua to enter self-imposed exile in Costa Rica, where he published a counterrevolutionary newspaper supplement in *El Nación (The Nation),* a Costa Rican daily.

Daniel Ortega's inauguration took place on the sixth anniversary of Pedro Joaquín's assassination. Quinto referred to the choice of dates by telling me that it was a "way of legitimizing the new government and," he added, "Ortega can be counted on to use my father's slogan, 'Nicaragua volverá a ser Republica' [Nicaragua will again be a Republic]."*

Quinto was intimately familiar with his father's thinking, and he believed that his Uncle Xavier's views were a distortion of Pedro Joaquín's liberal yet anti-Communist political tradition. He recounted some of that tradition to me during a May 1985 flight from Miami to Costa Rica when he spoke of what it was like growing up as Chamorro's son:

> When I was very small, my mother told me that my father was at "la aviación," but I did not know that that name described a prison. I thought that my father worked at an airplane factory. Once, when he was in prison, he made a small airplane with a propeller and sent it to me.
>
> My father did not have a lot of time with our family. Most of his time was spent in politics, but weekends with him were very special. We would take trips to Lake Nicaragua.
>
> My first child, a daughter, is named "Valentina" after a Mexican song that my father loved. He was so happy about the birth of my son [Pedro Joaquín VI]. Father had sent to Spain for the family coat-of-arms. He had key holders with the emblem made for everyone in the family. He wanted everyone to be proud of the Chamorro name.
>
> Once, at a party, when I was eight or nine years old, I saw the sons of Somoza. I thought I would not be welcome with the name "Chamorro," so I changed it for the day. My father became furious with me when he learned what I had done.
>
> Father was very oriented to the public—he rode a motor scooter to be in contact with the people. He would go to the slums on it.

---

*Tomás Borge, Sandinista minister of the interior, was a *La Prensa* distribution agent before Somoza García's assassination; Sergio Ramírez, vice president, contributed poems and prose; and Rosario Murillo, Daniel Ortega's common-law wife, had been Pedro Joaquín's secretary for twelve years. See Jaime Chamorro, *La Prensa: The Republic of Paper* (New York: Freedom House, 1989), 9.

Another quality was his unlimited courage. It is hard to believe how he faced problems—almost hair-raising. I remember one time a guy said he was going to kill him because of some offense he felt my dad committed. The man called my dad at home, and my dad told him that he should stop pestering him, but that if he wanted to see him he could come to *La Prensa*. (I was eighteen at the time.) He went to the newspaper early that day and, as usual, wouldn't ride with a chauffeur and wouldn't take me with him. I phoned *La Prensa* to warn the people there; everyone was worried. At the end of the day I went to *La Prensa* with a shotgun to escort my father home. He came out of the office alone, with only a newspaper in his hand. We went home together and quarreled. I said to him, "How can you be so silly going to work unarmed?" When we got home he took me out to a small pool in the backyard and said, "You think I'm silly?" Then he fired three bullets into the pool from the gun he had hidden in the newspaper. But ninety percent of the time he went about unarmed.

He really had a social conscience. Uncle Xavier and my father built a house on one of the islands in Lake Nicaragua. This house was poorly ventilated, and there were also so many mosquitoes and spiders. One day they decided to build a house for the custodian—a nice house—that would allow the breezes to enter. I asked my dad why we would not be using the new house instead of the custodian, and he answered, "Because he lives there every day, and we just go once a week."

One day my father called me to his office to discuss my development at *La Prensa*. He said, "I trust your principles, but not your emotions. I like what you're doing, but it's time for you to stop behaving like a salesman." He saw me more as a promoter because he just didn't know me that well.

It bothered him that for six years I wore an Afro and dirty blue jeans. When I returned from my studies in Canada, my father was very disturbed. I couldn't believe that my appearance would have bothered him so much. He took my large, Afro comb and put it on a low table outside. He said, "If the dog destroys the comb then you must get your hair cut; if he doesn't, you can leave it as it is." I put Tabasco sauce on the comb, but the dog still bent it out of shape. My hair got cut.

My father was very fond of action movies. He loved cowboy, mystery, and war movies. He enjoyed any movie where there was shooting. He loved listening to march music. He didn't like losing; he was a winner. He taught me how to play chess, and when I started beating him, he stopped playing me—the same thing in tennis. He was very competitive, and he could get forceful and quarrelsome, especially when he was under the influence. But if he hurt someone, he'd always apologize.

One day, driving from Matagalpa to Managua, my father and I passed a National Guardsman who was hitchhiking; my dad didn't stop to pick him up. I asked him, "Isn't he also your brother—your neighbor?" He was furious with me. I was getting too close to his own moral dilemma—the struggle between his hatred for the dictatorship and his religious feelings.

My father suffered big disappointments. People respected him, listened to him, but wouldn't follow him—wouldn't go to demonstrations he had organized—even the most oppressed wouldn't go.

Once, I accompanied him to a meeting at the barrio called "Ciudad Sandino" [Sandino City]. We were meeting there when it was prohibited. That was 1977, more or less. Few people showed up. He was so disappointed. I drove him home, and when he got to his room I knocked, entered, and said, "Father, I think that these people don't deserve your sacrifice." I was in the stage of being the protector, and I didn't want him shot. He cried and embraced me.

Many times he said that he was a failure—that he had not accomplished his goals—that he had not removed Somoza from power. Even the revolution was not worth the death of my father. The history of *La Prensa* and the Chamorros is so harsh. The people at *La Prensa* persevere even when others think it's hopeless, even after the bombing after Father's death. *La Prensa* will outlast the revolution. It may disappear for a few years, but it will come back.

Nicaragua Divided

Pedro Joaquín Chamorro Barrios will not leave the future of *La Prensa* to fate. He was chosen in February 1987 to represent the Nicaraguan Democratic Force (the contras) in the United Nicaraguan Opposition, its parent organization, later known as the Democratic Resistance.[2] In July 1988 he was removed when the contra military commander, Enrique Bermúdez, was named to it. Quinto, considered a moderate on that board, the descendant of the first president of independent Nicaragua, will continue to make his presence felt in Nicaragua's uncertain future. (During the summer of 1989, Quinto was supporting the opposition movement from his home in Miami.)

Xavier Chamorro shared the love and respect for his brother that Quinto had for his father. He had worked with Pedro Joaquín, following the death of their father, to build up *La Prensa* after returning from the United States with his engineering degree. When his brother was in jail and *La Prensa* was foundering, Xavier pitched in to manage it. His departure from the newspaper with 70 percent of the staff was a tremendous setback.

In his office at *El Nuevo Diario,* its walls covered with posters of his brother, Xavier described Pedro Joaquín to me by referring to a "landmark" in his own development. As a child he had been playing with little flags on the patio of his parents' home. He had been lining the flags up in a row, and Pedro Joaquín gently admonished him when he saw that he had not placed the Nicaraguan flag first in line: "First the flag of Nicaragua, then the others." Xavier believes that the Sandinista revolution is partially the result of his brother's long struggle. Modeling himself on the example his older brother set, Xavier has lent the credibility of the Chamorro name to *El Nuevo Diario:*

> I have innumerable memories of the struggle and the political involvement with Pedro Joaquín. My work now is a continuation of my work with him—I am following his example, striving for profound changes. But I agree that each member of our family is living what each believes to be the truth.
>
> Pedro Joaquín was very domineering in his thinking of what is "good." But the need to develop himself in all areas was what best characterized him. He never stayed static; he was always raising his social consciousness. He lived his ideals. Pedro Joa-

quín, more than anyone else, affected my development. There would be no *Nuevo Diario* if it weren't for Pedro.

In April 1986 Xavier offered to buy *La Prensa,* saying that the offer was his own and that it was not prompted by the Sandinista government.[3] The offer was rejected.

Jaime Chamorro, Pedro Joaquín and Xavier's brother, became co-director and general manager of *La Prensa* when his nephew, Quinto, went to Costa Rica. Jaime, his wife, Hilda, and their two teen-age daughters are traditional Catholics, deeply troubled about Nicaragua's future. The daughters have the same stoic outlook as their parents, but they miss the young men their own age who have gone off to the United States or elsewhere to avoid being drafted into the Sandinista army. After grace, said with bowed heads and encircled hands, followed by a tasty but carefully measured noontime meal (food is very scarce), Jaime spoke of his brother Pedro Joaquín: "Pedro was never a politician. He knew right from wrong, and when he had an idea that he thought was right, then that was that! For example, Carlos Holmann [married to sister Ana Maria] was like a brother to Pedro and lived in San Juan del Sur. Carlos had a nephew who was a Somocista, and the nephew proposed to Carlos that the nephew run for mayor. Carlos didn't like the idea, but thought that the nephew's election might somehow benefit the city. Carlos asked for Pedro's advice, and Pedro responded, 'If you support your nephew, I'll begin to attack you in *La Prensa.'* Pedro Joaquín was pluralistic in his ideas about the newspaper, but not in regards to morals."

Jaime said Xavier's offer to buy *La Prensa* was a strategy to get rid of the newspaper and an attempt by the government to eliminate one of the main problems the Sandinistas have with their foreign image.[4] In a *New York Times* interview, Jaime observed prophetically: "The Sandinistas want to sell an image that they are running a democratic, pluralist revolution. This helps them get aid from Europe and also protects them by giving them popular support in many places. The level of freedom that exists today is a tactic of the moment. Any day they can do away with *La Prensa* and the rest of the opposition."[5]

Carlos Chamorro, Pedro Joaquín's younger son, helped out at *La Prensa* after his father's death. He, like Quinto, was educated at Mc-

Gill University in Canada, but according to Quinto, Carlos was always first in his class, taking his studies very seriously. Pedro Joaquín used to tease him by calling him "Carlos Marx."

Family members consider Carlos to be the most introverted member of the Chamorro family. Tall like his brother, with a hairline resembling his father's, Carlos is much less accessible and approachable than are his brother and two sisters, Cristiana and Claudia. According to his aunt, Ligia Chamorro, Pedro Joaquín's younger sister, "Carlos had to have action. He had a tremendous feeling of frustration. Democratic ideals didn't offer enough of a solution to him so he gave his efforts to communism. If the Democrats in the United States could give their support to such a horrible man like Somoza, then the only way out was through a red flag." (Two of Ligia's five children are Sandinistas.)

The "action" that Carlos Fernando needed led to his position as director of *Barricada,* the newspaper whose masthead proclaims itself to be "The Official Organ of the FSLN." Although Quinto continues to have enormous respect for his brother for living his values in a consistent way, they are in political disunion.

On October 14, 1983, the Public Broadcasting System aired a program called "A House Divided" in which Hodding Carter interviewed Quinto, codirector of *La Prensa,* Carlos, director of *Barricada,* and their uncle Xavier, director of *El Nuevo Diario.* When Carter asked Carlos whether his father would have been a Sandinista were he alive, Chamorro replied, "I don't think my father would have been a Sandinista, a contra, or anything else. He would be totally honest with his position, trying to follow the interests of the majority of the Nicaraguan people." Carlos insisted that he is walking squarely in his father's footsteps: "We're journalists, but at the same time we're revolutionaries. *Barricada* is the organ of the FSLN. It has a political commitment. . . . I think the press has a tremendous role in terms of the education of the Nicaraguan people because we are the product of a society that was not a republic. There were absolutely no democratic traditions or institutions. More than fifty years of dictatorship did a lot of damage to the Nicaraguan people."

When asked on the same program whether or not the Sandinistas have substituted one form of tyranny for another, as critics often charge, Carlos replied that the charge was "not just unfair, but something that can't be proven. It is a popular government, with the support of a large majority of the people, which has given them a lot of benefits—agrarian reform, a literacy campaign. I don't think a tyranny would do such things." Carlos justified the censorship of *La Prensa* because "it goes beyond political opposition and has subordinated itself to the United States policy of aggression against Nicaragua." In a *New York Times* interview, he said, "We want an open society in which the right to dissent is guaranteed, but within logical limits."[6]

In an April 30, 1989, episode of "60 Minutes," Carlos admitted that he did not think his brother's dissent was within those limits. He said that Quinto had made a mistake when he got involved with the contras because they had been responsible for much of the damage Nicaragua has suffered. He believes that *La Prensa* has been the instrument of U.S. policies and that it has been manipulating his father's image: "They don't have legitimacy so they use my father's name." Carlos realizes that he has hurt his mother because she saw the family as Pedro Joaquín's "heritage," but he added that *La Prensa* is not the only receptacle of Chamorro thought. When reminded that his mother hopes that one day he "will see the light," Carlos, lovingly amused, responded, "Well, she's my mother."

Cristiana, who was shopping for her trousseau in Miami at the time of her father's death, became an editorial writer at *La Prensa*. Politically she is at odds with her sister, Claudia, a Sandinista, who left her position as second-in-command at the Nicaraguan consulate in Cuba to become ambassador to Costa Rica. Cristiana spoke to me of the influence her father had upon her life:

> I have not yet assimilated everything. He was my friend, teacher, father. There were so many examples he set for us. He left the door open for questions. I still feel a great respect for him and try to live his ideals. Only by living with him could one measure his richness as a human being.
>
> Father was so liberal in his ideas, but he always respected contrary ideas. Each child had his own ideas, and we always learned to have an enormous respect for each other. Claudia, for example, believes her way is best. My brothers really believe that what they're doing is right.

The best part about growing up in my home were the communications. He was very attentive—he wanted to know our real thoughts. But he was also a great joker and teaser.

At times he could be very rigid, but more than anything else, he was affectionate. He was strict, but allowed us to make our own mistakes and learn from them. He trusted us.

Since we were small we lived with the idea that one day he would die. It was a normal theme. I had a dread of that day. I feared that I would feel hate for everyone, but when they killed him, I felt peace because of the loving response of all the people. It was a miracle that he lived as long as he did.

In my father's earliest letters to his parents, he wrote that he feared that he had almost too much love for his country. He was profoundly Christian. He lived his Christianity.

He had hopes for President Carter, but he always believed in independence from the United States. He was opposed to U.S. policies with Somoza. He never got the changes he expected from Carter.

He instilled in all of us a deep love of country, a dedication to free thought, and respect for the thoughts of others.

We often spoke of current events at home during lunch. We were either laughing or very serious. He often invited friends home to lunch. He loved young people and welcomed them to our home.

He was very democratic at work and at home. He would ask for different opinions. When he made a decision it was after it had been discussed with others.

My hope is that my children will grow up in a free country, and my place is in Nicaragua.

In May 1985 Cristiana's sister, Claudia, was visiting at their mother's home in Managua. Although Violeta is troubled by Claudia's identification with the Sandinistas, she welcomed her as if there were no barriers between them. She was eager, however, for Claudia to have an opportunity to talk about her father because she thought the young woman had not yet opened herself to anyone about what her father's life and death had meant to her. The young, intense woman was visibly moved as she softly described the legacy she received from her father:

Family Legacy

I was the daughter of Pedro Joaquín Chamorro. I am his daughter. I have present at every moment the awareness that I have a very great responsibility. If each Nicaraguan could have had the kind of historic and human responsibility that I have there might be a different situation here. I don't argue with my brothers, mother, with no one. Everyone has to interpret those responsibilities for himself.

I had such a good relationship with my father. I had always thought that the day that they would kill him I would feel hatred. But when that day came, even though there was much pain, I knew that this had been his destiny—that this was the death for which he had been predestined. One cannot always live to see the results of a struggle. At times it is necessary to surrender life.

From that moment of acceptance, I had to continue living with the values that he respected. I had to live with the examples he had shown us. He was much more than a father. He was a brother, teacher, friend, and companion. I learned so much from him, but not everyone can apply principles in the same way. From him I learned the most important thing—how to be a human being. I learned that each person is the "master of his own fear."* I learned how to be master of my own fear. It is not easy because it means you have to be authentic above all else, conscientious and effective. From him I learned to love life, to love my neighbor.

He was a model of conscientiousness, correctness, and integrity. He saw the world full of corruption, but he never stopped being a real Christian. He made his life a practice of that Christianity. He wasn't the kind of Christian who is content with just praying in church.

There were many times when he tried to impose his standards on us—he could behave like a grand dictator—but, generally, he was a man with whom you could reason.

I discovered my father when I was very small. (I think fa-

---

*In an interview on Costa Rican television, after Chamorro said negative things about Somoza, the interviewer asked him why he wasn't afraid to say such things. He replied with a Mexican proverb: "Yes, I am afraid, but everyone is the master of his own fear."

thers have to be discovered.) I discovered him when I had to face the confusing nature of life with all of its struggles. He had to be gone so much of the time. I needed to find out what was happening to him. One time I found the book that he wrote in prison. It was banned in Nicaragua, and possibly forbidden for us at home, too, because I have the impression that he wanted us isolated from the knowledge of how difficult and painful life had been for him. Perhaps he wanted his children to live the life he had not lived. He wanted the world to be different and wanted his children to see this other world, so he protected them from what he lived. At least this was my experience.

So I found his book and read it one day, secretly, and found something I'll never forget—a letter that he wrote to my mother when he was in the mountains, when he thought he was going to die. At the end of the letter he put a message that speaks of the dedication she would have to give their children after he was gone, and in one sentence he wrote that we, and other children like us, are the country, for whom one must be ready to die.

And it was there that I found my father. There, that I knew who he was, and that I had an obligation to him. I never told him that I had read the book, or what that book signified for me, but I told him after they had killed him.

I have been asked innumerable times what my father would have done if he were alive. And the answer that I always give is that "my father did what he had to do," and what I learned from him is that I must do what I have to do. If I did not, I could not use his name.

I have chosen the path that he showed me, the path of the country and of the poor; I also chose another path that he showed me—of making my life a practice of Christianity. I have found in this revolution the opportunity to make my life a Christian one. The revolution has given me such a grand capacity for loving. It's like a large platter of love from which one helps himself at breakfast, lunch, and dinner, with more love left over at the end of the day.

The revolution has also taught me something else—respect— respect for even the greatest enemy. And I learned to have respect for them, even before love, and so at times my road is difficult because not many people learn to respect in this manner.

When he died, I had to continue living—to learn that there is still a lot of love in the world. I surrendered all of my efforts to the revolution, and in the revolution I found everything I had already dreamed of.

The pages of my father's story, written with his own blood, represent the history of the revolution. There are many people who want to transform those pages into something worthy. He now has an eternal place in our history. He wasn't a Sandinista, but he was a man who fought a parallel fight against the dictatorship.

I am with this revolution. I have a firm conviction that this is the alternative for the Nicaraguan people. I am sure that on the way mistakes are made, that inadequate methods are sometimes chosen, that impulsive measures are taken, that solutions are decided upon that do not correspond to the problem. But we should be aware that the revolution is made by men and men make mistakes. I am basically convinced that the goal of the revolution is good; that the struggle is good; that here there are no personal ambitions; that here there are no party interests.

I had never studied Marxism, but I am a Marxist. I do know that before one becomes a Marxist, one must develop a conscience. The problem is not one of communism or Marxism—the problem pertains to conscience. The problem is not one of conflict between the East and the West, but of misery. The problem is not any of those things that people try to blame. The problem regards a valiant country that was sold out, and that a people, for the first time in their history, want to be truly Nicaraguan.

My father had an extraordinary sensitivity—one of those men born so rarely who have so much capacity to achieve so much, but to whom the world does not give permission.

I remember my father during the difficult years (when I was already aware of his involvements) complaining about those men who were abandoning him, of those who claimed they were his friends, but who were much more concerned with their own political ambitions than with their friendship with my father. They abandoned him when he had dialogue with the Socialists or with the Communists, and those same men wanted to identify with his name after he died. Those same men are also the ones who are now against the people.

I can also tell you that he had friends—brothers to him, who were his brothers up until the end, and who continue to be brothers of the people. I can mention some names: Dr. Rafael Córdova, an engineer, who was a member of the governing junta and is now a representative on the General Assembly; Dr. Roberto Hurtado, who was president of the Supreme Court until a short time ago, and who has been named ambassador to France; Licenciado [equivalent of a master's degree] Reynaldo Antonio Téfel, who is director of the Nicaraguan Institute of Social Welfare; Dr. Juan Ignacio Gutiérrez Sacasa, who is a medical doctor and now director of the military hospital.

When the interview was over, Claudia went to the phone on her father's desk to call a cab. She greeted the dispatcher with the term "compañero," the equivalent of "comrade" but with the softer Spanish connotation of "friend." The dispatcher, not liking the greeting, hung up on her.

Claudia married Edmundo Jarquín, Nicaragua's ambassador to Spain, on September 23, 1986. The wedding was celebrated on the day that would have been Pedro Joaquín's sixty-second birthday.[7]

In a political world distant from Claudia's, Violeta Barrios de Chamorro lives in the unpretentious but spacious house that she and her husband built twenty years ago when they could afford to leave the home of Pedro Joaquín's mother, Doña Margarita de Chamorro. Like so many houses done in the Spanish style, it has a courtyard filled with dense, tropical plants. There is a picture of Pope John Paul II on the heavy, wooden entrance door. (The picture of the pope has become a symbol of anti-Sandinista protest ever since his March 1983 visit to Managua when he scolded Trappist priest Ernesto Cardenal for his participation in the Sandinista government.)

When she is at home, Violeta spends most of her time in a small, sun-filled sitting room that opens up to a small patio where she keeps the Saab in which Pedro Joaquín was gunned down on January 10, 1978. In the garden, against a tree, is propped a piece of the fuselage of the airplane that carried him and his men to Nicaragua from Costa Rica during the 1959 invasion. Still very slender, her black hair now a blend of salt and pepper, Violeta spoke of how it was to raise her children during the years her husband was in prison:

> When Pedro had to go to jail during the Somoza dictatorship, I did not want to inculcate hatred within my children, nor rancor, because they were very small, and I don't believe that a small child can understand such things, so it was better not to embitter their lives.
>
> Pedro, the oldest, asked me, "Where is my father?" I answered, "At the airplane factory." (The prison was called "La Aviación.") He asked, "What is he doing there?" "Making airplanes," I replied.
>
> So I mentioned to Pedro Joaquín, when he could have short visits, what I had told our son, and he made a small airplane out of tongue depressors for him and sent it as a gift.
>
> I never told our son anything because I decided that when he could understand what was happening in this country—what was the Somoza dictatorship—that he could come to his own conclusions. When he was eight, I enrolled him in a boarding school so that he wouldn't be exposed to ugly rumors, but could be studying and playing.
>
> Claudia and Cristiana were very small children at that time, and Carlos Fernando was born during a different period—when Pedro Joaquín had been released in a general amnesty, but was kept under house arrest. I didn't tell them anything until they were sixteen, and then I gave them the book, *Bloody Stock: The Somozas,* which their father also wanted them to read—the first book that he wrote when he fled from this country.
>
> In general, that was my way of teaching them. I don't think young children, who can't even talk, should have to hear, "Who is Carlos Fonseca?"* or "Who is Marx?"

---

*Carlos Fonseca was a founder of the Frente Sandinista, killed in battle in 1976, a revolutionary hero to the Sandinistas. His picture is frequently used in grade-school primers and is associated with the teaching of revolutionary vocabulary.

When Violeta's children were in elementary school, at times they would be sitting next to Somoza children in their classes. Her children would come to her and ask her how they should treat them. She would advise them to speak to the Somozas, to be friendly with them. She never told them of the menacing threats that she and her husband frequently received. When the children were troubled or sad she would send them to speak with their father. It was he to whom they usually went with their serious problems.

Violeta reminisced about their weekend outings. Pedro Joaquín had bought a sailboat when they were financially able, and they and their friends would sail on Lake Nicaragua. Her husband loved to make intricate charts for these excursions. He loved the natural beauty of Nicaragua—its lakes, volcanos, rivers—and when he was not in jail, he would try to enjoy it at every opportunity. The photos on the wall of Violeta's sitting room attest to the zest for life they had as a couple.

Many of the rooms of the Chamorro home hold objects and memorabilia pertaining to Pedro Joaquín. The sailboat has a room all to itself. His motor scooter, on which he regularly rode into the poor parts of town, leans against a courtyard wall under a large poster of him with the words "Freedom of expression is the right of people and not the gift of governments." His den is as it was when he lived—every inch covered with ancestral pictures, photos of Pedro Joaquín fighting bulls at family picnics, photos from courtship years. A glass case holds the bloodied clothes he wore on the day of his murder. The bar, located at the far end of his den, is decorated with mementos from *La Prensa* and a plaque that sarcastically reads, "In this house, we are all friends of Somoza." The den remains the family's gathering spot because of its inviting, dark coolness, its circle of rocking chairs, and the lingering presence of Pedro Joaquín.

Violeta said that despite her husband's sense of humor, he was very methodical. He would get home from work about five-thirty in the afternoon and would frequently want to go to the movies. Although Violeta disliked the Westerns and war films her husband preferred, because many of the brutal scenes reminded her of the mistreatment he experienced in prison, she accompanied him rather than stay home by herself.

Violeta and Pedro Joaquín had been married twenty-seven years when he was killed. According to Emilio Álvarez Montalván, who related that Chamorro had many female admirers who would have loved to have had affairs with him, he had been true to Violeta throughout their marriage. Álvarez Montalván mentioned, in Violeta's presence, that once her husband had been sorely tempted and was about to enter into an affair with an attractive young woman who had been after him, but at the last moment he backed out with the words "I'm not cut out for this sort of thing."

Álvarez Montalván described Violeta as a strong woman and added that Pedro Joaquín had always preferred women who were strong like his own mother. Once, his friend recalled, when Pedro Joaquín was small, he was bothered by a nervous facial tic. His mother, Doña Margarita, hit him with a stick and the tic never reappeared.

Violeta, who had not been politically active during her marriage, became the only woman on the first revolutionary junta after his death. She remained with the junta for only a short time. Although she left ostensibly for health reasons, she confided that she simply did not like the direction the Sandinistas were taking. She continues to visit *La Prensa* every day while Pablo Antonio Cuadra and her brother-in-law, Jaime Chamorro, direct its operation.

Violeta said that *La Prensa* strives to retain the same ideological orientation that her husband brought to it when he joined his father in its direction in 1948, when he was only twenty-three years old. She remains unyielding in her opposition to the political bent of the newspapers directed by her son, Carlos, and her brother-in-law, Xavier. Before going to bed each night she commends herself to Christ, to the Virgin Mary, to Pope John Paul II, and to her husband, whose spirit is alive within her.

That spirit could be seen at the March 1986 conference of the Inter-American Press Association held in Salvador, Brazil. There Violeta addressed two hundred journalists, speaking out against Nicaraguan press censorship. According to the Brazilian newspaper *O Estado de São Paulo (The State of São Paulo)*, Violeta spoke with clarity, dignity, and emotion and, in return, received enthusiastic applause.[8]

On June 25, 1986, the U.S. House of Representatives, in a 221 to 209 vote, approved $100 million in military and nonlethal aid for Nicaraguan antigovernment guerrillas. Two days later the International Court of Justice (World Court) ruled that the Reagan administration had broken international law and violated Nicaraguan sovereignty by aiding the antigovernment rebels.

The Nicaraguan government ordered the closing of *La Prensa* on June 26 because the paper had tried "to justify the U.S. aggression." The *La Prensa* editors called the decision "a black moment for the people of Nicaragua."[9]

On July 29, 1986, a "Letter to Ortega" appeared in the *New York Times*. In it Violeta condemned the Sandinista regime but stated that the crisis in Nicaragua must be solved by Nicaraguans:

President Ortega,

As chairman of the board of directors of *La Prensa,* I was not greatly astonished to hear your recent statement that I deserve to be sentenced to 30 years in jail after being tried by the people's anti-Somocista tribunals.

I say that I listened to these words without surprise, because I am now accustomed to hearing you speak. Your expression is confused and contradictory, full of the kinds of passion not befitting a head of state.

If you so desire, I will happily turn myself in to the authorities, so that they may apply the jail sentence with which you are threatening me. In this way, I will be proudly following the example of my husband, Pedro Joaquín Chamorro Cardenal. Imprisonment was the only way the previous dictatorship, led by Gen. Anastasio Somoza Debayle, could deal with him.

How quickly you have forgotten my strong nationalist position. Remember that in 1979, in San José, Costa Rica, I was the only one who opposed any resolution of the Nicaraguan problem that included the involvement of foreign countries. What I said then I say now: the grave crisis afflicting Nicaragua must be resolved among ourselves, the Nicaraguans, without the interference of Cubans, Soviets or Americans.

You will never convince anyone that I am a traitor to my country, nor that I received money from the Central Intelligence Agency, nor that I am part of the Reagan Administration's terrorist plan. These falsehoods have been repeated so often that now nobody believes them. Commander Ortega, the same thing is happening here in Nicaragua as in other countries under Communist dictatorship: because there are so many lies every day, no one will believe you on the day when you say something true.

I also heard in your speech that you seem to like the idea of doing with me what the Americans did with citizens of Japanese descent during the greatest armed conflict in history: imprison everyone who is slightly suspicious in concentration camps.

This is already under way, Commander Ortega, by means of repression and the banning of all contradictory opinion. Your Sandinista party has already created a great concentration camp in Nicaragua. But the Nicaraguan people are not losing their liberating spirit and will never lose it even in the worst of the gulags your mind is able to conceive.[10]

CHAPTER 7

STANDING FIRM

Violeta received a two-line note from the Sandinista government on June 26, 1986, informing her that *La Prensa* was closed indefinitely. She was ordered to pay the wages of all the workers in full, according to their contracts. In order to pay those costs, the directors of the newspaper decided to sell some of its assets.[1]

Foreign journalists observed these hardships. In September 1986 Violeta received the Louis Lyon Award from the Nieman Foundation of Harvard University. Twenty national and international journalists nominated her for "conscience and integrity in journalism." Mark Etheridge, managing editor of the *Charlotte Observer,* then a Nieman fellow and chair of the awards committee, cited "Violeta's efforts to keep the free press alive in Nicaragua." He noted that *La Prensa* "resisted repression from every quarter" and, although Violeta broke with the Sandinistas, "she did not flee Nicaragua like so many contratypes."

Not silenced by the closure, Violeta, in the winter 1986 issue of *Foreign Affairs,* exhorted that "western democracies need to be decisive and firm in coordinating their efforts to demand a civilized government in Nicaragua, based on the right to free elections and respect for the fundamental rights of man."[2]

She also explained that "*La Prensa* supported the diplomatic efforts of the Contadora group of nations from their inception" and expressed disappointment that the representatives from Mexico, Panama, Colombia, and Venezuela "failed to come forward with a proposal that

94

offers acceptable and workable solutions to achieve internal democracy in Nicaragua." She added:

> Perhaps if these gentlemen of goodwill would meet one day in Nicaragua and see the military hospitals of one side or the other, filled with sixteen-year-olds torn apart by machine guns, missing arms and legs, blind, or with fate uncertain even after extensive operations, they would then demand that an agreement be signed guaranteeing freedom for Nicaragua.
>
> Behind this war—a civil war between Sandinista soldiers recruited against their will and Nicaraguan "contras" on the other side—there is a profound tragedy in which a whole people is impoverished by the loss of a great treasure: their freedom.
>
> That is why we of the free press, loyal to our principles, believe that before all else the country must be returned to normalcy. We believe the appropriate first step must be to initiate the national and international dialogue we have desired for so long, for which my husband was struggling up to the moment he gave his life, for which we all have struggled with profound conviction for sixty years past.[3]

The 77th World Interparliamentary Conference met in Managua on April 27, 1987. Violeta took advantage of this gathering to publicize the government's abuses. *La Prensa* distributed a posterlike notice that called for "worldwide solidarity" against the decision to close the newspaper. On the poster was a photograph of Pedro Joaquín and a message denying the existence of a parliamentary system in Nicaragua, in spite of the fact that there was a general assembly composed of representatives in proportion to the votes their parties received in the general election. The same message was sent to the embassies of the countries represented at the conference.[4]

A few days later thirty armed soldiers came to the newspaper's plant, detained and interrogated the directors, and, according to Violeta, threatened to jail them. A search was conducted, and the plates and film used to print the poster were confiscated.

Violeta expressed her dismay in an opinion piece in *The Times of the Americas:* "The Sandinista government, not satisfied with having arbitrarily brought about the closure . . . has continued a series of aggressions against the newspaper which I think the whole world should know about." She concluded her article with a reminder that *La Prensa* is "fighting against a deceitful, seductive, false ideology that can trick exploited peoples."[5]

Impatient with the U.S. military solution exemplified by Oliver North and his supporters and with the lack of political will of the Central American nations in solving their problems, Oscar Arias, president of Costa Rica, proposed a solution for ending the conflict in Central America that he hoped would have special impact on Nicaragua.

His ten-point plan called for "a ceasefire in countries with conflicts, the cessation of all foreign assistance to armed groups and new elections in Nicaragua in exchange for amnesty for political prisoners and the initiation of dialogue among affected governments and their internal oppositions." In Guatemala City on June 7, 1987, he said, "As long as there is no peace agreement in Central America, each one of the countries will feel the necessity to import more and more arms, to live defensively, but we believe that this folly can be replaced by maturity and intelligence."[6]

The Iran-contra hearings kept the U.S. public enthralled or disgusted during the summer of 1987. Oliver North became an instant hero for some and the symbol of misguided patriotism for others. In the hearings the public learned that the 1985 sale of arms to Iran to benefit the contras was considered a "neat" idea by Admiral Poindexter and by those who thought it a stroke of genius to get around an intransigent Congress.

The majority of a joint congressional panel did not think the arrangement neat and issued a summary of the hearings on October 13. They found no direct evidence that the president was responsible for the sale of arms and the diversion of funds, but the panel agreed that "the President created or at least tolerated an environment where those who knew of the diversion believed with absolute certainty that they were carrying out the President's policies." Other statements reported by Philip Shenon in the *New York Times* were equally condemnatory:

If the President did not know, he should have known.

While the President was denying any illegality, his subordinates were engaging in a cover-up.

96

The actions of these individuals do not comport with the notion of a country guided by the rule of law. But the President has yet to condemn their conduct.

Officials viewed the law not as a boundary for their actions but as an impediment to their goals. When the goals and law collided, the law gave way.

The lies, the shredding, all the attempts to rewrite history, all continued unabated even after the President authorized the Attorney General to find out the facts.

Congress was told nothing, and what it was told was false.

Enough is clear to demonstrate beyond doubt that members of the President's National Security Council staff were out of control, that fundamental policies of governance were disregarded, and that the rule of law was subverted.

A minority group on the panel disagreed with the tone of the majority report, based on their belief that the Boland Amendment, which was designed to restrict aid to the contras, did not apply to North, Poindexter, and other members of the National Security Council. These members also disagreed with the use of the term "cover-up," because it connotes criminal behavior and, according to them, no crime was involved.[7]

Meanwhile the staff of *La Prensa,* unsure of the practical value of the Arias plan, which was signed by the Central American presidents in Esquipulas, Guatemala, on August 7, worried about the newspaper's survival. While closed, its employees had been urged, according to the *Village Voice,* "to go into exile and join the contra radio station."[8]

In an attempt to be viewed favorably while world leaders were studying the Arias plan, President Daniel Ortega visited Violeta at her home on September 19, 1987. He told her of the government's willingness to allow *La Prensa* to reopen with the understanding that there would be a certain degree of censorship.

Violeta, in the company of her daughter Cristiana, brother-in-law Carlos Holmann, and Pedro Joaquín's sister Anita, told President Ortega that the only condition under which *La Prensa* would be reopened was that of complete freedom from censorship. The group requested, too, that their freedom to publish be extended to the Catholic radio station and all other censored media.

After one hour of discussion, Ortega agreed that the newspaper could be reopened without censorship, assuming that its governing board would exercise journalism in keeping with the laws of the state of emergency. This would prohibit *La Prensa* from coming out in favor of the loan of $270 million President Reagan planned to request from Congress to keep the contras a viable fighting force. (On October 13 President Oscar Arias was awarded the Nobel Peace Prize for his peace initiative, an award that helped doom Mr. Reagan's request for aid.)

The Sandinista government would make Soviet newsprint available to *La Prensa* even though it had previously accused the management of having received financial assistance from the CIA. (Carlos Chamorro, in a MacNeil/Lehrer television interview on November 4, 1987, made the same charge.)

Jaime Chamorro acknowledged that the National Endowment for Democracy, a U.S. government–funded organization, had promised to help the paper reopen with ink and supplies worth $98,000, bringing to $254 million the amount *La Prensa* had received from that organization since 1980.[9] The Brazilian magazine *Imprensa* never referred to the agency but simply explained that "*La Prensa* survived thanks to financial help from the North American government that has already delivered 254 million dollars for the purchase of equipment." *Imprensa* quoted Jaime Chamorro as saying that the American assistance would not interfere with the paper's editorial line: "Reagan may even like what we say, but we would have already said it."[10]

President Reagan did not like the words of President Arias when Arias spoke to a joint session of Congress about his plan on September 22, 1987. Arias urged reconciliation in countries "where brothers are set against brothers." As if predicting that the shadow of contra aid would continue to loom, he cautioned Congress: "We will not fall into a trap set by someone who shows us a calendar every day, anxious to bury the last hope. We have opened the door to the rule of reason in Central America and to reconciliation and dialogue."[11]

La Prensa opened with a diminished staff and few distribution trucks (the fleet had been sold to pay salaries and meet expenses) on October 1, 1987. The banner headline read: "The People Triumphed."

Underneath the headline was a large photograph of Pedro Joaquín.[12]

Readers of the 200,000 copies sold read the article in which Violeta explained her fears that *La Prensa* could be closed again when the censors decided they didn't like the truth. She added that the FSLN would use the newspaper's reopening as propaganda to prevent the U.S. Congress from providing more aid to the contras.

An opening-day editorial convinced readers that *La Prensa* would not be striking bargains with the government and prepared readers for any future closing: "We reject being an object of manipulation for the good of the political interests of the FSLN, and we remain steadfast in our position that we will never accept the brutal FSLN censorship that was imposed on this newspaper for four and one-half years before it was closed. The day in which the FSLN tries to impose censorship on *La Prensa* will be the day it immediately closes."

In the same editorial, the editors of *La Prensa* tested the Sandinistas' understanding of the concept of a free press: "*La Prensa* reappears in the middle of peace efforts that we welcome and endorse. Six and one-half years of war have carried this country to a state of prostration, and the people are paying with hunger and pain for the political mistakes and deviations of the FSLN."[13]

The editorial continued with a plea for total amnesty for political prisoners, reconciliation and dialogue with the contras, and the total removal of the state of emergency. Using the newspaper in the battering-ram style of Pedro Joaquín, the editorial writers gave the Sandinistas notice: "In the name of the Nicaraguan people, *La Prensa* today tells the FSLN that Nicaraguans never wanted, do not want, nor will ever want a totalitarian dictatorship in the Communist style. If 45 years of struggle against Somocismo did not tire the Nicaraguans, 8 years of this new attempt to subdue them likewise hasn't the least chance of success. Nicaraguans have never submitted to a tyranny, no matter its name. Our history and daily actions prove it."[14]

Pablo Antonio Cuadra, codirector of *La Prensa*, slapped the hands of those who would make promises and not keep them:

> It is not our responsibility to support the Sandinista Front nor to commune with Marxist-Leninism. To the contrary, it is our journalistic responsibility to oppose the FSLN. The majority of

our people do not want a party with totalitarian privileges nor a State that owns and controls all, but a live and active democracy within a structure of law and justice.

For us, the revolution has been sidetracked and arrested. Our responsibility is to return it to its democratic purpose and return political dominion to the people, the guarantees and freedoms that are now abused and unlawfully held by one party. We don't want the gains of the revolution to be lost, just the opposite: Rescue them and rescue the economy and the culture, not for the State, but for men and women. Our responsibility is the Nicaraguan people.[15]

Wilbur Landrey, foreign editor of the *St. Petersburg Times* and chairman of the Inter-American Press Association's press freedom committee, commented on the reopening, "There must be few occasions when a government and a newspaper have set out such an understanding in writing, and each could conceivably interpret the words in different ways." Landrey offered the caveat that the reopening of *La Prensa* did not equal press freedom in Nicaragua: "As in Chile, a state of emergency is still on the books under which Ortega could take everything back tomorrow."[16]

In fact, the Sandinistas did temporarily revoke their agreement with the newspaper when, in July 1988, they closed *La Prensa* for fifteen days because its reporting "endangers national security and national defense, slanders government leaders, incites violence and calls for civil disobedience and the subversion of public order."[17] (*La Prensa* had reported that there had been police brutality during a July 10 protest rally in the town of Nandaime. Opposition leaders were imprisoned after the demonstration and thirty-nine remained there until December 1988.)[18]

In the *Columbia Journalism Review,* Michael Massing, a contributing editor, analyzes the content of *La Prensa* and concludes that many of the articles were provocative, designed to test the government. In early 1988 *La Prensa* reprinted an article from a Costa Rican newspaper that attributed Pedro Joaquín Chamorro's assassination to elements of the Sandinista Front—a charge, according to Massing, they could not back up and one that was highly inflammatory considering that

Chamorro is viewed as a hero by Sandinistas and anti-Sandinistas alike.[19] In an ironic twist, Massing saw a truck unloading 300-kilogram rolls of newsprint from the Soviet Union during a visit to *La Prensa*. He wrote that the trucks came all day, delivering a total of 700 tons: "Thus did Soviet generosity help keep the flame of press freedom alive in Nicaragua."[20]

Francisco Goldman doubted that *La Prensa* had been using its freedom as would become what he dubbed "the most famous of Third World newspapers." In an August 1988 *Harper's Magazine* article, the contributing editor reminds readers that the *New York Times* mentioned *La Prensa* 263 times in the past four years.[21] Goldman evaluated the content of newspapers from Guatemala, El Salvador, and Honduras, nations the United States considers to be democracies, for their freedom from censorship. He notes that those newspapers did not need a censor because armies, poverty, and fear do the job. He claims that Nicaragua had the freest press in Central America because of the vehemence permitted on both sides of the ideological chasm. On one side of that rift is *Barricada,* under the directorship of Carlos Chamorro, which touts the party line and accuses all Sandinista opposition of taking advantage of the political openings that have occurred to destabilize the government. On the other side is *La Prensa,* which, despite its stature as a Nicaraguan institution, has become, according to Goldman, "relentlessly ideological, propagandistic, one-sided, sensationalistic, negative, and even dishonest."[22]

Goldman explains that *La Prensa* can get away with its unsubstantiated claims against the government because the rest of the world believes that press freedom is alive and well in Nicaragua as long as this newspaper is published, no matter what it prints. For example, he cites an article that accused a Sandinista army patrol of the grotesque torture and massacre of a peasant family. According to Goldman, the newspaper did not name a witness but accepted the word of the victim's aunt who came to *La Prensa* to make the denunciation.

Goldman marvels at the differences among the major newspapers of Central America. In Guatemala, El Salvador, and Honduras, for example, articles criticizing the military would not be tolerated, but in Nicaragua they are common. Nicaragua has to prove to the world that it is not a totalitarian state and so allows *La Prensa* to get away with journalism that would be quickly squashed in the other countries. *La Prensa* takes advantage because it knows it is the symbol of the Sandinistas' stated intention to democratize if only the United States would relegate the contras to the dust pile of failed foreign policies. Goldman believes that *La Prensa* has been audacious because of the moral and financial backing of the U.S. government through the CIA, the National Endowment for Democracy, and the Oliver North network.[23] Jaime Chamorro defended the outside help. He wrote that the Sandinistas would not sell *La Prensa* the foreign currency needed to buy supplies nor, when the money was available, would they transfer it to the paper's suppliers. "Thus," wrote Chamorro, "we were grateful for a grant for which the Sandinista government had ironically created the conditions."[24] The Chamorros did not receive direct financial aid from the United States. Instead, wrote Chamorro, the money was sent to their suppliers who then shipped such supplies as ink and chemicals. (Readers who want detailed information on the nature and extent of Sandinista censorship of *La Prensa* should read Chamorro's 1989 book, *La Prensa: The Republic of Paper.*)

A more objective voice may cause both *Barricada* and *La Prensa* to review their policies. With the financial help of a foundation funded by the Dutch government, a group of young Nicaraguan journalists began *La Cronica,* a newspaper "pledged to independence and balance." Stephen Kinzer of the *New York Times* writes, however, that the paper, which will be the only one in Nicaragua not run by a Chamorro family member, has "an unabashed anti-Sandinista tint."[25]

Although Nicaraguans have much to gain if the tenets of the Central American Peace Accord are carried out, many are skeptical. Dr. Emilio Álvarez Montalván, who recently joined the editorial board of *La Prensa,* expressed his doubts in an interview with Flora Lewis of the *New York Times:* "We have no history of democracy, no experience of opposition here. There is the regime, and the rest are always bought out or squelched. It is the same now despite the revolution."[26]

Nevertheless, on January 10, 1988, the tenth anniversary of Pedro Joaquín Chamorro's assassination, ten thousand people participated in a mile-long march in Managua to register opposition to the Sandinistas.[27] The opposition is enormous but splintered. As of November 1989, there were twenty-three parties, of which twenty-one were legally recognized, including the Communist—a fact that surprises many North Americans who assume the Sandinistas are all Communists.

For three months in 1988 the Sandinistas sponsored TV propaganda they hoped would bolster their own position. Viewers watched images of Violeta, Pablo Antonio Cuadra, and Jaime Chamorro interspersed with scenes of contra carnage, a tactic used to link *La Prensa* with the U.S.–sponsored war. How did these cruelly sensational programs affect Carlos and Claudia Chamorro, and will such devices force them to choose unequivocally between family and state?

Leadership acceptable to all the opposition groups is desperately needed if they hope to unseat the Sandinistas. If Cardinal Obando y Bravo, held in great esteem by so many, will not assume that post, Flora Lewis suggests that Violeta de Chamorro would be the natural choice, her health permitting: "She is known to be firm, nonpartisan, non-vindictive, unsullied by the past, brave, honest and reliable." Lewis likens her to Corazon Aquino of the Philippines and speculates that the Sandinistas might even consider Violeta as the spokesperson for the opposition: "They know how her husband's murder galvanized the country."[28]

The Sandinistas will have to do more than contend with Violeta as opposition spokesperson. On September 2, 1989, she was chosen as the National Opposition Union's candidate to run against Daniel Ortega in the February 25, 1990, elections. There are eight other contenders. According to information in a *Washington Post* news bulletin, picked up by the *Milwaukee Journal*, "Chamorro is virtually the only opposition figure in Nicaragua whose stature and prestige rivals that of Ortega."[29] If elected, Violeta plans to release all prisoners in jail because of anti-Sandinista activities, abolish the military draft, and dedicate herself to "humanizing" Nicaragua which she regards as "destroyed."[30]

It is too early to predict the political future of Nicaragua. As these words are written the Sandinistas are laying the ground rules for the February 1990 elections. The opposition groups are jockeying for media access, government financial support, and a say in the formation of the election regulations. Both the Sandinistas and the opposition believe they know what is good for Nicaragua.

Soviet writer Vasily Grossman has questioned the concept of "good." He asks, "Is there a common good—the same for all people, all tribes, all conditions of life? Or is my good your evil? Is what is good for my people evil for your people?"[31] Somoza's good was not good for the majority of the people, and they rebelled. Is the good that the Sandinistas bring more desirable because they claim to have had the majority of Nicaraguans in mind when they developed literacy programs, health clinics, and agrarian reform and reduced the infant mortality rate after the revolution? Does that good outweigh the hardships borne by others who have experienced press censorship, educational indoctrination, the submission of the arts to governmental themes, and the scarcity of basic commodities?

The members of Pedro Joaquín's family have chosen justice as their good, but because they describe justice differently, their means of achieving it are inimical to each other's purposes. There is no doubt that each passionately loves Nicaragua as Pedro Joaquín did; each has dreams of prosperity and peace for the country; each reflects a deep sense of mission. As Nicaraguan poet Mario Cajina-Vega wrote of Pedro Joaquín, his children and other family members believe his spirit lives on in them:

No muere:
Tiene por cuerpo al Pueblo
Y por espiritu a la Libertad[32]

(He does not die:
The people are his body
And freedom is his spirit)

CHAPTER 8

PERSONAL REFLECTIONS

A t the time of my first visit to Nicaragua, three years after the 1979 "triumph," as Nicaraguans refer to the end of the Somoza regime, the people were hard at work rebuilding their country. The old political and economic structures that dated back to colonial times still existed, and Nicaraguans needed time and money to break out of them.

Under the Somozas more than half of Nicaragua's 2.5 million people lived in hopeless poverty. There was widespread malnutrition, and close to half of the registered deaths were of children under five.[1] People did not benefit from their own work, and their absolute powerlessness kept them hungry and poor. The poorest Nicaraguans were landless. The few that did have land had parcels that were too small to meet their families' nutritional needs. Large landowners often forced peasants to work small mountainous plots where little could be grown.

Before the 1978–79 revolution in which 50,000 Nicaraguans lost their lives, children in the coffee-growing regions did not attend school. They helped their mothers pick coffee in the cold and damp. They ate little. Many children died from childhood diseases that in richer countries would have been considered insignificant threats. Because their mothers were undernourished themselves, breast milk was limited, and mothers tended to use overly diluted infant formula mixed with contaminated water. The ensuing chronic diarrhea left children with little resistance.

Conditions in the coffee plantations were traditionally atrocious. Several families would sleep on one platform in a barn. Hygiene was nonexistent. Meat was eaten once only—at the end of the harvest. Workers were forced to spend their money at the camp store and would end up owing the manager their meager wages.

After the revolution the Sandinista government attempted to diversify the workers' nutrition. The addition of cheese and fruit could considerably improve their diet, which was typically beans and tortillas. In addition to providing workers with better nutrition, an effort was made to employ men for the full year, which is difficult to accomplish because of the seasonal nature of coffee and tobacco farming. Men were out of work after the short season. In 1981 tobacco crops were being rotated with corn so that the soil was being used on a year-round basis. Children were still working on the farms in 1981, but instead of working six days a week without any schooling, they worked half-day shifts so that they could attend the schools that were brought to each farm.

Health clinics were also established on the farms. Some of the big ones had doctors; smaller ones had nurses. After finishing five years of medical school, doctors had to contribute one or two years of social service. Public health clinics throughout the country sponsored educational programs for pregnant women.

Throughout the country literacy education was receiving a great deal of attention. Shortly after the revolution a campaign took place that sent thousands of high school students to rural areas for months at a time as literacy instructors. Many of these youngsters were from very wealthy homes and had never experienced physical hardship. As a result of this intensive program, the illiteracy rate was reported to have decreased from 50 to 12 percent. The students who participated in the endeavor returned to their families and schools deeply satisfied at having contributed to a cause that they knew would have a great impact on Nicaragua's future.

Cubans were helping in the literacy campaign as they were in the health clinics. They kept low profiles and many Nicaraguans shunned them, afraid that the Cubans might try to spread their political ideology. In 1981 there were approximately 1,500 Cuban teachers in Nicaragua, and 1,300 Nicaraguan students were in schools in Cuba.

UNICEF sponsored five pilot centers that specialized in early stimulation of deprived infants and young children. The organization was also working with ten- to twelve-year-olds who had little environmental preparation for school. According to Jilma de Herodocio, director of special education for the country—a position that did not exist before the revolution—the war caused trauma and anxiety that is believed to have resulted in serious learning problems among the children. Of the seven thousand children who registered in the schools in 1980, one year after the revolution, thirteen hundred of them did not pass their grade.

The problem of dropouts was also enormous. Students who experienced the war were unable to conform to the school functions required of them. Most children in the city of Estelí, for example, participated in constructing the blockades that were used to obstruct Somoza's National Guard. They helped to carry furniture from their homes and asphalt from bombed-out roads to build the barricades. Many children served as couriers and assumed responsibilities well beyond those normally expected at their age. Many witnessed the killings of family members.

A discussion of the early postrevolutionary period would be incomplete without some comment on the role of the church. Churches throughout Nicaragua carried posters on their bulletin boards that urged Christians to unite—to do their part in the reconstruction of their country. Documentation for social activism was offered from the Old and New Testaments.

Members of the Oxfam-America group, with whom I traveled, talked with Father Ernesto Cardenal, Sandinista minister of culture. Father Cardinal described the identification that priests, nuns, and church workers had with the ideals that prompted the revolution. He saw no other role for the church than putting principles into action by working to better the living conditions of the poor. By working to promote human dignity among them, the religious in Nicaragua were making their lives a practice of Liberation Theology—that is, the liberation of the poor from subhuman and oppressive living conditions.

There was another side: Through conversations with people from the upper middle class and talks with a university professor, I learned how fearful some people were that Communists might be taking over their country. While admitting that they had earlier identified with the revolution, they were vocal in their denunciation of communism. They said that some Sandinistas had confiscated houses and cars and that this practice had fed their fears. They were afraid to invest their money in Nicaragua, and the resulting flight of capital further weakened the already precarious economy. Reinforcing their suspicions, *La Prensa* had been shut down on a few occasions because of its negative commentaries about the junta.

Some people welcomed President Reagan's hard line toward the Nicaraguan government. Others, even though critical of the Sandinistas, believed that Reagan's position would drive their nation closer to Cuba and communism. "They sent it to Cuba" was the comment frequently overheard in the stores when women could not find the items they came for.

Women's groups were emerging. In Managua I spoke with a leader of one of these groups who said that the role of women was slowly changing. Illegitimacy was a big problem before the revolution. There were no laws to protect children born out of wedlock or their mothers. "Now," she said, "fathers are compelled to be financially responsible for their children." I also learned that in certain barrios where so many men and youths had been killed during the war, most of the households were headed by women. As the poster in the office of this women's association proclaimed, the new Nicaraguan woman was being "constructed" along with the new Nicaragua.

Although Nicaragua was still very poor, Amnesty International reported that during their mission visits of 1979 and 1980 at least the torture and terror that existed during the Somoza era were gone.[2] And the country was producing more staple foods—up to 15 to 25 percent over prerevolution highs. Over twelve thousand formerly landless rural families had received land since the victory over Somoza. Tens of thousands more were to receive land titles under the 1981 Agrarian Reform Law. In the first eighteen months of the new government, inflation was reduced from 84 to 27 percent. Unemployment dropped from 40 to 16 percent.[3] The slogan I saw painted on the door of a humble country house best describes the attitude of many Nicaraguans in 1981: *"Con trabajo y sudor haremos una patria mejor"* (With work and sweat we will make a better country).

I returned to Nicaragua in 1985, after deciding to write a book about Pedro Joaquín Chamorro, whose essays I first read during my 1981 visit in memorial editions of *La Prensa*.

Quinto, Pedro Joaquín's elder son, drove me to the San José airport the day after I interviewed him en route from Miami to Costa Rica. I carried medicines and musical tapes from him to his mother. Shortly after our meeting, Quinto became information officer for the contras.[4]

"Welcome to the Land of Sandino" read the sign that greeted the passengers on the Copa airline flight from San José to Managua. As I entered the customs areas and met the blank stares of guards and the intimidating mirrors at the passport control desks, I was reminded of an earlier trip to Poland. Fortunately, my encounter at customs was uneventful and, after changing sixty dollars for córdobas at the official rate of twenty-eight to the dollar (which all U.S. citizens had to do upon entering the country), I got a cab and headed for the Intercontinental Hotel.*

There was much traffic on the road to the city. People hung from crowded buses. Convoy trucks carried soldiers. Posters along the road cheered the development of socialism. Children were begging— something I had not seen in 1981. I told the cab driver why I had come back to Nicaragua, and he told me how much the people still revered the memory of Pedro Joaquín. He was "a man of the humble," said the driver. He pointed out the exact location of the assassination, where Pedro Joaquín's car had been rammed before he was gunned down, and the monument on the street corner dedicated to him. It was a large,

---

*In February 1988 the Sandinista government replaced its currency at an exchange rate of ten córdobas to the dollar. By December the dollar brought 4,500 córdobas, and, as of June 1989, the dollar exchanged for 26,250 córdobas. The current economic situation means that consumption has been cut by more than 70 percent and per capita output is now below that of Haiti. See Mark Uhlig, "Nicaraguan Study Depicts Economy in Drastic Decline," *New York Times,* 26 June 1989, A1; and Peter Pasell, "For Sandinistas, Newest Enemy Is Hard Times," *New York Times,* 6 July 1989, A6.

semicircular form that had been defaced by the popular Sandinista graffiti, "FSLN."

I later learned from Violeta that Avenida Kennedy, the street on which her husband was killed, was to have been changed to "Avenida Pedro Joaquín Chamorro," but she believed that the Sandinistas would never get around to it because of her strong vocal opposition to the ruling regime.

In the hotel dining room, my cream of tomato soup and rum and coke cost nearly twenty-two dollars at the official exchange rate. During the meal I met a twenty-three-year-old student from the University of Wisconsin at Madison—a student of archaeology who had been on a "dig" in Belize. He knew where I could get a better exchange rate for my dollars and drew a map for me.

There was no light in the bathroom of my $65-per-night quarters, nor was there air conditioning. I could not get a call through to my family and spent a sweaty and restless night. In the morning I saw about fifty bare-chested young men running around the enormous field in front of the hotel. They wore fatigue pants and appeared to be in some very lax form of military training.

My breakfast of bread, fruit, and coffee came to $10.85. I was going to have to do something about exchanging my money if I was to remain in Nicaragua long enough to complete my work. Determined not to keep spending the way I had, I followed the map the student gave me. After a long walk in the hot sun, I found the house where a housewife gave me 500 córdobas to the dollar. I later learned that, with the right contacts, one could get up to 700. Everyone was trying to get dollars because they were needed to buy anything of value. In order to accumulate more dollars for foreign exchange purposes, the state operates an import store like those in Cuba and Poland, where dollars may be exchanged for scarce imported products.

I had wanted to make contact with Violeta, but the phones were not working, so I decided to hire a cab for 800 córdobas per hour. On the state's exchange that fee would have been formidable. Now it was quite affordable.

I will never forget entering the Chamorro home and my pleasure at meeting Violeta. She offered me an ice-cold glass of coconut milk and suggested that I let the cab driver go. She informed me that "they" cut off the phones at will, but that she had been expecting me. She offered to let me use her shower, a proposal I had not heard since I was a Peace Corps volunteer in Peru. I did not know then that my hotel water had been cut off after I left and that this conservation measure was practiced twice a week. While I had bathed before the cut-off, unfortunately I had not filled my tub for an evening bath—much needed in torrid Managua.

That evening, after a sponge bath with soap and bottled water, I pondered the many hours of conversation with Violeta. She lived among her memories and memorabilia when she was not busy at *La Prensa* or involved in some other important cause, and admitted to having trouble sleeping at night. She took me back to the bedroom that she had shared with Pedro Joaquín. I saw where she had listened to him predict his own death and funeral.

She was very proud of her seven grandchildren and commented on how hard it was to find room for all of their portraits in a house already covered with photographs. I was surprised to learn that there had been a fifth Chamorro child, Maria de los Angeles (Maria of the Angels), who died shortly after birth. While she was showing me the photographs, I had the impression that she was saying "Look how very happy this family has been." It was as if those mementos could somehow ward off the rapid and frightening changes she sees in Nicaragua.

In my hot room I remembered the dark coolness of Pedro Joaquín's study where we retreated after hours at *La Prensa,* enjoying rum and cokes, known as "Nica libres," while seated in rocking chairs. We ate sweet green grapes from vines that Pedro Joaquín had planted years ago. After a delicious, informally served dinner, we drank tea. I wondered if Violeta preferred the beverage or if she, like so many Nicaraguans, could not buy coffee because the best was being exported to lower the huge foreign debt inherited from Somoza.

Violeta said that she would not leave Nicaragua, no matter how difficult things became. "They will have to kick me out," she added. She goes to the United States every few months to see a doctor who treats her for osteoporosis, but this travel has become more difficult as there are restrictions on how many dollars can be taken out of the country.

Violeta invited me to accompany her to the cemetery where she goes on the tenth of every month to lay flowers on her husband's grave. As we walked among the graves, she noted how ill tended the cemetery was and how in Costa Rica the cemeteries are so beautiful. She was reminded of her conversations with Pedro Joaquín in which she wanted to discuss their burial plans and how he refused to participate.

I stood with her as she placed flowers on the grave, and we said a prayer. Walking back to the car, she told me how the Sandinistas had raised their flags all over the cemetery until the people protested. She told her chauffeur to take me to my hotel, and she went on to a meeting to raise money for a reception for Archbishop Obando y Bravo, who was to be named cardinal the following week in Rome. I couldn't help but think that she was a strong woman, a woman who knew her own mind and projected an image of proud self-confidence.

On the way back to the hotel, the chauffeur complained about how difficult it was to find medicines, and that at least under Somoza they were available. "Now," he said, "there's nothing in the drugstores." He added that people had become used to U.S. brands and were reluctant "to accept those from Communist countries."

Even at 10:00 P.M. it was hot. There was a dance under way on the floor above me with booming rock music that alternated with torrid Latin rhythms. From the first floor came mariachi music from the restaurant known as the Mexican Corner. I fell asleep after having a scotch, from a bottle I had brought with me, mixed with warm, bottled water.

In the morning I enjoyed the buffet breakfast in the hotel restaurant. It cost 250 córdobas, or 50 cents. I felt guilty. Either I felt cheated by an exchange rate of 28 córdobas to the dollar, or I got 500 to the dollar and felt I was cheating.

I tried to make an appointment to see Carlos Chamorro, Pedro Joaquín's younger son. When I called, everyone was very polite, addressing me as "compañera Patricia," but the only way I could have seen him was to have gone in person to fill out a form stating my reasons for wanting the interview. (In addition to being the director of *Barricada,* Carlos served as director of "Agitation and Propaganda.") A committee would have determined whether I could meet with him, and if the decision was positive, I would have had to return another day. If transportation was an easier thing, and if it had not been so

112

hot, I might have been more inclined to pursue the matter. Violeta also tried to get him to see me but to no avail.

I needed no committee review at *La Prensa*. A word from Violeta was sufficient. After interviewing many of the employees, I also learned something about the practical side of living in Sandinista Nicaragua. There was no toilet paper in the rest room. The employees kept their own rolls in their desks.

One afternoon I was trying to get back to the hotel after having spent time with Xavier Chamorro, Pedro Joaquín's brother, the director of *El Nuevo Diario*. I waited for over an hour in the hot sun for a bus or cab. Nothing stopped. The buses that passed had people hanging out the doors, straddling the bumpers, or clinging to the luggage racks on the top. Half the buses in the city had broken down, and all the parts must be imported. This situation makes for a long workday for the average Nicaraguan who must rely on public transportation.

If they are lucky, workers can flag down a collective taxi. Fortunately, one stopped for me before picking up two women, each carrying a sick child. One of the children was about five months old. He sucked from warm formula in a plastic bag. He looked frail and was burning with fever. The other woman carried a little girl over her shoulder who was four years old. The mothers asked to go to a clinic. We entered one of the poorest parts of Managua—excruciatingly poor and hot.

The driver dropped the women off at a rehydration center where mothers are encouraged to bring children who have chronic diarrhea. In 1981 there were billboards all over the country that warned parents that "children with diarrhea can die." Other signs urged women to breast-feed their babies to protect them against the debilitating bouts of diarrhea that can occur when mothers use contaminated drinking water to prepare formula for which there is no refrigeration. I did not see any health education signs during my 1985 visit; the war effort had priority over social needs.

I noticed that as the driver stopped to drop off passengers or pick up new ones, he would gently ask, "Son, where are you going?" Despite the sticky heat, passengers would squeeze together to accommodate one more who would reply, "Thank you, love."

I thought to myself, "So what if the Sandinistas are taking sixty dollars from us at the airport and are only giving us twenty-eight córdo-

113

bas to the dollar. It's the least we can do, especially since nearly everyone discovers the parallel market. The Nicaraguans are defending themselves from U.S. hostility and, as a result, are having to live like this." I felt ashamed of our pugnacious policies and felt great solidarity with their poor.

Emilio Álvarez Montalván, Pedro Joaquín's friend, had said that Nicaragua gave birth to its own dictators but that the United States had incubated them. In a sense we are responsible for the emergence of the movement that our government is seeking to destroy. If Sandinismo is the child, then Somocismo was the womb, placenta, and umbilical cord that connected it to the United States. We have been trying to abort our unwanted child.

On Mother's Day I decided to see what was happening in the churches. I had read so much about religious persecution in the U.S. press, and I wanted to see for myself if Sandinista policies were interfering with the right of Nicaraguans to worship. Alejandro, the driver, turned out to be solid and reliable, a father of five children who was worried about his oldest boys because they were reaching the age for serving in the militia.

We went first to El Cerrito (the Little Hill), where I thought Archbishop Obando y Bravo would be saying eight o'clock mass. The archbishop had been supportive of the Sandinistas but now was firmly opposed to many of their policies. To the archbishop's dismay, they had closed the Catholic radio station, which they believed was becoming a source of counterrevolutionary ideology, and had exiled priests who had become too vocal in their opposition to the government. No one was at the cathedral, but there were a few cows grazing in its front yard. We decided to return for the eleven o'clock mass.

The driver asked whether I would be interested in visiting a park where the Sandinistas had been displaying some very old armaments that had been restored. As I wanted to see more of the city, I agreed. The park was surrounded by ruins—crumbled houses from the 1972 earthquake. Many trees had been planted in an attempt to beautify the park, but the houses could not be concealed. There were no tanks or weapons, but I did see three small children emerge from one of the ruins. The two boys and a little girl, all undernourished, were about five or six, but they looked younger. One child's black hair was begin-

to the contras has not forced them to reach out to the Soviet Union or Cuba, as critics of U.S. policies toward Nicaragua believe. Ligia, Jaime, and Hilda treated each other with respect and tenderness. Their strength derives from their fierce loyalty to family, faith, and country. They continue to pray that Divine Providence will change the course of events in their homeland.

Torn between my respect for the Chamorros who oppose the Sandinistas and my understanding of those who support the regime, I tried to convey my ambivalence in a phone call to my husband. Just as I mentioned the increasing poverty, an outrageously loud noise boomed into my ear from the receiver, and my connection was cut off. A few minutes later the operator came on the line to tell me that we had been reconnected. My husband and I finished our conversation. After we said our good-byes, I called the hotel operator to object to what I presumed to be eavesdropping and censorship. He apologized but added that if someone had been monitoring the call, it had not been done from within the hotel.

This is the sort of thing that evokes my sympathy for those who are opposed to the current regime, even though I recognize the Sandinistas' achievements in the early years of the revolution and have been appalled by the major role the United States has taken in the destabilization of Nicaragua's government. I cannot ignore the fact that while we have antagonized the Sandinistas, the effects of our hostility have been borne most heavily by the poor. And I cannot excuse our arrogance in having snubbed the peace initiatives of the Contadora nations of Colombia, Venezuela, Panama, and Mexico, as well as the advice of most other Latin American countries. While we maintained an embassy in Managua, we supplied a surrogate army and engaged in "covert" operations against Nicaragua. By encouraging confrontation rather than negotiation, our policies were contributing to the militarization of all of Central America.

During my second visit to Nicaragua, I spent most of my time with people who were opposed to the Sandinistas. Yet I never heard one suggest that Nicaragua's problems would be solved by continued war. They believed that fifty thousand lives lost in the revolution against Somoza had been enough.

Chamorro would have detested the Sandinistas' censorship, and he would have considered the 1986 closing of *La Prensa* an act of betrayal of the ideals of the revolution. Pedro Joaquín had a profound respect for the power and potential of "the word." He closed his book *Richter 7* with these thoughts: "The word has died from the same blow that is killing man. The word is man's most perfect expression . . . because in order to write, one needs to reflect, to stop and use all of one's senses. . . . The word is a kind of secret, a mysterious key . . . so that when it dies, as it is doing now, when it is abolished, censored, dishonored, eradicated as if it were malaria, man himself dies or anguishes in the recesses of his mind. It is not a coincidence that these processes begin with the death of the word. First, we stop writing and reading, then speaking with others, and finally, we stop thinking."[6]

The Sandinistas should have read the preceding paragraph before they developed, in preparation for the February 1990 elections, a new media law that, according to Edward Seaton, vice president of the Inter-American Press Association, is not democratic because it places the media "at the service" of whatever the state deems to be in the national interest. Although the law does not mention fines or confiscations, and does not permit permanent shutdowns or prior censorship, it does allow for suspension of publication for up to forty-five days if a state of emergency is declared. It also permits "temporary suspensions" for up to thirty days for periodicals and ten days for newspapers and radio stations. Seaton recounted the infractions for which penalties are imposed in the *Wall Street Journal:*

> Penalties are imposed for infractions that include a laundry list of violations: many pure generalities, ranging from information infringing "state security" to failure to promote "the correct use of the Spanish language." Between these extremes come libel; material "contrary to national integrity, peace and public order"; failure to respect "the dignity of individuals . . . the beliefs and traditions of the Nicaraguan people . . . patriotic symbols and Heroes and Martyrs." The press also is required to develop "the spiritual and cultural level of the people."[7]

Although Pedro Joaquín would have decried the silencing of *La Prensa* and the new media law, he would not, I believe, have approved of U.S. military intervention. Just as he did not want the Sandinistas to misuse the name and history of Sandino, he would not have wanted Nicaragua's future to be directed by the United States, a position that did not endear him to some U.S. politicians. He would not have been our man in Managua.

He would have deplored the indoctrination that exists in Nicaraguan schools and the pervasiveness of revolutionary rhetoric in the children's texts. He would have protested the way in which the arts have become pillars of the revolution and would have wanted the revolution to culminate in a liberally educated people who would know that ignorance and fear breed irrational behavior.

He would, however, have admired the original good works of the Sandinistas, especially their gains in reducing the dreadful infant mortality rate that was Somoza's legacy. Pedro Joaquín would have applauded their success in reducing the illiteracy rate—a goal to which he and his newspaper were dedicated. He would also have championed the movements to build health clinics and housing for the poor.

On the other hand, he would have been the first to stand up against the mistreatment of the Miskito Indians—a people he respected greatly as a result of his visit to their settlements at a time when most Nicaraguans did not concern themselves with their existence, much less their welfare. The Sandinistas have since acknowledged that errors and abuses occurred in their dealings with the Miskitos and have sought to rectify them through the Constitution (see appendix, chap. VI).

Pedro Joaquín would have been saddened by the mass recruitment of sixteen- and seventeen-year-old boys for service in the militia. He would have felt desperation upon seeing the billboards that praise mothers for their willingness to give up their young sons to defend Nicaraguans against Nicaraguans and their U.S. backers.

Looking toward the future, Edgar Chamorro, Pedro Joaquín's second cousin and former contra leader, told me the following in an April 1987 interview: "Pedro Joaquín will become in twenty to thirty years for Nicaragua what Sandino is for the Sandinistas. And the future of democracy in Nicaragua will hinge on the principles that Chamorro represents. He became a civilian fighter. In the long run, he'll be considered more of an inspiration and example because he used civilized means, having given up the rifle."

In May 1989 Oliver North, who had not given up his hope in the rifle, was found guilty of three of twelve criminal charges for his involvement in the Iran-contra arms-for-hostages affair. The jury accepted North's argument that he was merely following orders, despite the warning from Judge Gerhardt Gesell that they understand that no one had the authority to cause North to break the law. North said he knew that lying to Congress was wrong, but that he didn't know it was illegal. The jurors accepted the argument that North had not intended to do something illegal when he lied to Congress. They dismissed five other charges using the same rationale. They did, however, find North guilty of accepting an illegal gratuity, shredding government documents, and constructing a false chronology to mislead the investigators led by independent counsel Lawrence Walsh.[8]

On July 5, North was sentenced to a three-year sentence, which Judge Gesell suspended. The judge put North on probation for two years and fined him $150,000.[9] (North could have gotten ten years in jail and a $75,000 fine.) North will be barred from seeking federal office, a hope his followers relished, and he will be denied his $23,000-a-year military pension.

Instead of organizing fund-raising activities for the contras, North will now have to do 1,200 hours of community service in a new Washington, D.C., antidrug program. The sentence frees North to continue to earn $25,000 for each speech, enabling him to pay off his fine after six such addresses. About these speeches Judge Gesell said: "Your notoriety has given you many difficulties but it also has made you a rich man. . . . You can continue to inflame the myth with which you have supported yourself, or you can turn around and do something useful. The future is up to you."[10]

The judge reminded North that he was "a low-ranking subordinate working to carry out initiatives of a few cynical superiors," and told North that he had "responded certainly willingly and sometimes even excessively to their requirements." "Thus," said the judge, "you became . . . part of a scheme that reflected a total distrust in some constitutional values."[11]

Had Oliver North understood the seriousness of his behavior? Judge Gesell expressed his doubts when he told North, "Along the way you came to accept the view that Congress couldn't be trusted." He added, "I believe you still lack a full understanding of how the public service has been tarnished." The judge justified his lenient punishment by telling North that a jail sentence "would only harden your misconceptions."[12]

On August 7, 1989, the five presidents of the Central American nations signed an agreement in Tela, Honduras, calling for the dismantling of the estimated ten thousand contras based in Honduras by December 5. The United Nations will supervise the voluntary surrender of arms in cooperation with the Organization of American States.

I have been working on this book, in one form or another, for eight years, as long as the United States has been supporting the contras. I am hopeful that as the production of this book ends, an era of misplaced militarism directed against Nicaragua will also end.

There will be those who say that the contras forced the Sandinistas to make concessions. At what price to the poor of Nicaragua? And what of the price paid by the people of the United States who know that their government once again engaged in imperialist activity against a sovereign Central American nation?

My son and grandchildren will study our military intervention in Central America. I pray that they will not allow their government to do what my generation has allowed. I hope that their government will cooperate with the people of Central America rather than try to dominate them, that the U.S. Constitution, which has been a model for Central American governments, will mitigate our own egoism, reminding us that the liberties we want for ourselves are also desired by others.

The Central American people have paid a severe penalty for our historic support of dictators in the region. Much of the turmoil there is the product of a foreign policy that is still inspired by an attitude of superiority toward our southern neighbors, an attitude that has quashed needed change in order to preserve our economic and political interests. Change will come. We've seen the boiling pot overflow in Nicaragua. The kettles boil in El Salvador, Guatemala, and Honduras. We provided much of the fuel. Will we continue to try to put down revolutions by using more force? Are we sufficiently mature to ally ourselves with those who seek democratic change even though it disturbs powerful social and economic traditions? We were too slow in Nicaragua; we relied on outdated, short-sighted responses. The United States played an integral part in the history leading to the revolution in Nicaragua; we now have an opportunity, however late it has been recognized, to assist in the rebuilding of this nation by positive means.

You would be misled if, reading this, you conclude that I am pro-Sandinista. I am for the Nicaraguan people and for the legacy left by Pedro Joaquín Chamorro. We've reduced too many political situations to a good-guy/bad-guy analysis. We have failed to see the fabric of a country, the people, their culture, religion, language, and history. Our media-shaped minds prevent us from dealing with complexities. I want my country's policies to reflect the highest ideals befitting the oldest enduring democracy on earth. The contras never did fit that standard.

Pedro Joaquín's children see long struggles before them. Two believe that the Sandinistas represent everything their father fought: oppression, censorship, and totalitarianism. Two others believe that the new government is the vehicle by which they can act upon their inherited values of justice and compassion for the poor, and they are optimistic that the 1987 Constitution will guarantee that these values will predominate in Nicaraguan society.* In common, however, they hope that one day Nicaragua will at last control its own destiny.

---

*In addition to the individual's right to food, shelter, education, and worship, the Constitution guarantees the right to information. Articles 66, 67, and 68, which deal with press freedom, may be found in the appendix.

APPENDIX
The Constitution of 1987

Chapter III: Social Rights

Article 66: Nicaraguans have the right to truthful information. This right includes the freedom to seek, receive, and publish information and ideas whether through oral, written, or pictorial means, or through whatever mechanism they choose.

Article 67: The right to inform is a social responsibility, and it should be exercised with strict regard for the principles established in the Constitution. This right is not subject to censure, but to the responsibilities subsequently established in the law.

Article 68: The means of social communication are in the service of national interests.

The State will promote the public's access and that of its organizations to the media, and it will prevent these from being subject to the monopolistic economic power of any group.

The existence and function of public, corporate, and private media will not be subject to prior censorship and will be subject to that which is established in the law.

Chapter VI: Rights of Communities
on the Atlantic Coast

Article 89: The Atlantic coast communities are an integral part of the Nicaraguan people and, as such, enjoy the same rights and have the same obligations.

The Atlantic coast communities have the right to preserve and develop their cultural identity within the national unity, to found their own social organizations, and to administer their local business in accordance with traditions.

The State recognizes the communal form of property ownership in the lands of the Atlantic coast communities. It also recognizes the possession, use, and benefits of the waters and forests of the communal lands.

Article 90: The Atlantic coast communities have the right to free expression and preservation of their languages, art, and culture. The development of their culture and values enriches the national culture. The State will create special programs for the exercise of these rights.

Article 91: The State has the right to make laws which assure that no Nicaraguan will be the object of discrimination for reason of language, culture and origin.

Constitución Politica, *La Gaceta Diario Official* (Managua), 9 January 1987, 43, 46–47.

NOTES

Chapter One

1. "World Beat," *Atlas World Press Review* (January 1978): 6.

2. Violeta Barrios de Chamorro, "Su Unica Bandera," *La Prensa,* 11 January 1981 *Literaria Suplemento Conmemorativo*, 1,7.

3. Viron P. Vaky, speaking before the Subcommittee on International Affairs, Committee on Foreign Affairs, House of Representatives, Washington, 26 June 1979.

4. "Shotguns Silence a Critic," *Time,* 23 January 1978, 55–56.

5. "New Rioting Erupts in Nicaragua Capital," *New York Times,* 13 January 1978, A1.

6. Carlos M. Vilas, "El sujeto social de la insurrección popular: la Revolución Sandinista," *Latin American Research Review* 20, no. 1 (1985): 119–45.

7. John Padgett, "Who Killed Pedro Chamorro?" *Soldier of Fortune* (March 1985): 52–57. Quotes from p. 57.

8. Jaime Chamorro Cardenal, *La Prensa: The Republic of Paper* (New York: Freedom House, 1989), 66.

9. Ibid., 75.

10. Ibid.

11. *Mexico City News,* quoted in Bernard Diederich, *Somoza: American-made Dictator* (New York: E. P. Dutton, 1981), 155.

12. Pedro Joaquín Chamorro, *Estirpe Sangrienta: Los Somoza* (Mexico City: Editorial Diógenes, 1957), 14.

13. "Espero el golpe que ya Ud. me tiene destinado," *La Prensa,* 10 January 1981.

Chapter Two

1. Bernard Diederich, *Somoza and the Legacy of U.S. Involvement in Central America* (New York: E. P. Dutton, 1981), 153.

2. *La Patria de Pedro* (Managua: La Prensa, 1981), 80.

3. Gregorio Selser, *Sandino* (New York: Monthly Review Press, 1981), 15.

4. Diederich, *Somoza and the Legacy,* 4.

5. Vicente Saenz, "Pasado, Presente y Porvenir de Centroamérica (II)," *Cuadernos Americanos* (Mexico City) 6 (November-December 1944): 40–41.

6. *La Patria de Pedro,* 81.

7. *La Prensa Cincuentenario* (Managua: La Prensa, 1977), 24.

8. Ibid., 130.

9. "Vida y libros de P. J. Ch. por el mismo," *La Prensa,* Literaria Suplemento Conmemorativo, 11 January 1981, 1.

10. Diederich, *Somoza and the Legacy,* 9.

11. Ibid., 12.

12. Ibid.

13. *El Universal* (Mexico City), 28 December 1926, quoted in Selser, *Sandino,* 55.

14. Diederich, *Somoza and the Legacy,* 13.

15. Pedro Joaquín Chamorro, *Estirpe Sangrienta: Los Somoza* (Mexico City: Editorial Diógenes, 1957), 59.

16. "Nicaragua: Murder at the Crossroads," *Time,* 5 March 1934, 16–17.

17. Diederich, *Somoza and the Legacy,* 15.

18. Ibid., 19.

19. William Krehm, *Democracies and Tyrannies of the Caribbean* (Westport, CT: Lawrence Hill, 1984), 110–11.

20. "Nicaragua: Murder at the Crossroads," *Time,* 5 March 1934, 16–17.

21. Diederich, *Somoza and the Legacy,* 20; Krehm, *Democracies and Tyrannies,* 111.

22. Chamorro, *Estirpe Sangrienta,* 61–62.

23. Krehm, *Democracies and Tyrannies,* 122.

24. Chamorro, *Estirpe Sangrienta,* 142.

25. *La Patria de Pedro,* vi.

26. Charles D. Ameringer, *The Democratic Left in Exile* (Coral Gables, FL: University of Miami Press, 1974), 206.

27. Chamorro, *Estirpe Sangrienta,* 28.

28. Ibid., 182.

29. Diederich, *Somoza and the Legacy,* 48.

30. *La Prensa,* 30 September 1956, 1.

31. Chamorro, *Estirpe Sangrienta,* 28, hereafter referred to by page numbers in parentheses in the text.

32. "Shotguns Silence a Critic," *Time,* 23 January 1978, 55–56.

Chapter Three

1. Pedro Joaquín Chamorro, *Estirpe Sangrienta: Los Somoza* (Mexico City: Editorial Diógenes, 1957), 251.

2. Ibid., 254.

3. Ibid., 257.

4. Ibid., 21.

5. For detailed description of April 1959 rebellion, see Pedro Joaquín Chamorro, *Diario de un Preso* (Managua: El Pes y la Serpiente, 1981); Charles D. Ameringer, *The Democratic Left in Exile* (Coral Gables, FL: University of Miami Press, 1974), 269–79; and Charles D. Ameringer, *Don Pepe* (Albuquerque: University of New Mexico Press, 1978), 159–61.

6. Chamorro, *Diario de un Preso,* 176, hereafter referred to by page numbers in parentheses in the text.

7. Ameringer, *Don Pepe,* 159.

8. *La Patria de Pedro* (Managua: *La Prensa,* 1981), 85.

9. Ibid., 17.

Chapter Four

1. Eduardo Crawley, *Dictators Never Die* (New York: St. Martin's Press, 1979), 124.

2. Ibid., 125.

3. Pedro Joaquín Chamorro, *Estirpe Sangrienta: Los Somoza* (Mexico City: Editorial Diógenes, 1957), 141.

4. Ibid., 140.

5. *La Patria de Pedro* (Managua: *La Prensa*, 1981), 89–90.

6. Bernard Diederich, *Somoza and the Legacy of U.S. Involvement in Central America* (New York: E. P. Dutton, 1981), 79–82.

7. "Luis Anastasio Somoza Is Dead; President of Nicaragua Seven Years," *New York Times*, 15 April 1967, H12.

8. Crawley, *Dictators Never Die*, 141.

9. Pedro Joaquín Chamorro, *Los Pies Descalzos de Nicaragua* (Managua: *La Prensa*, 1967), 8.

10. Pedro Joaquín Chamorro, *Nuestra Frontera Recortada* (Managua: *La Prensa*, 1970), 20.

11. Penny Lernoux, "Nicaragua's Miskitos: Strangers in a Familiar Land," *The Nation*, 14 September 1985, 202–6.

12. Pedro Joaquín Chamorro, "Sandino Nacionalista pero nunca Comunista," *La Prensa*, 10 January 1981, 2.

13. Pedro Joaquín Chamorro, *Richter 7* (Managua: El Pez y la Serpiente, 1976), 10.

14. Ibid., 11.

15. Horacio Ruiz, *La Prensa*, 1 March 1973.

16. *La Patria de Pedro*, 149–50.

17. Diederich, *Somoza and the Legacy*, 100.

18. Pedro Joaquín Chamorro, "Espero el golpe que ya Ud. me tiene destinado," *La Prensa*, 10 January 1981, 4.

19. *La Prensa*, 24 June 1974, quoted in Diederich, *Somoza and the Legacy*, 101.

20. Diederich, *Somoza and the Legacy*, 102.

21. Ibid.

22. Crawley, *Dictators Never Die*, 153.

23. Ibid.

24. Ibid.

25. Ibid., 153–54.

26. Pedro Joaquín Chamorro, *Jesús Marchena* (Managua: El Pez y la Serpiente, 1975).

27. Grafton Conliffe and Thomas Walker, "The Literary Works of Pedro Joaquín Chamorro," *Caribbean Review* 7, no. 4 (October–December 1978): 46–50.

28. Gregorio Selser, *Sandino* (New York: Monthly Review Press, 1981), 43–44, 161.

29. Ernesto Cardenal, "Pedro Joaquín Chamorro revolucionario," *Nuevo Amanecer Cultural,* 11 January 1981, 2.

30. Crawley, *Dictators Never Die,* 5.

31. Ibid.

32. Charles D. Ameringer, *The Democratic Left in Exile* (Coral Gables, FL: University of Miami Press, 1974), 255.

33. Chamorro, *Estirpe Sangrienta,* 11–12.

34. Conliffe and Walker, "The Literary Works of Pedro Joaquín Chamorro," 46–50.

35. Press release, Office of Public Information, Columbia University, New York, 31 October 1977.

36. Pedro Joaquín Chamorro, "Palabrería y burguesía," *La Prensa,* 10 January 1981, 2.

Chapter Five

1. Alan Riding, "Newspaper of Slain Nicaraguan Editor Leads Strike," *New York Times,* 1 February 1978, A3.

2. "Nicaragua Imposes Emergency Law," *New York Times,* 29 January 1978, L14.

3. Alan Riding, "Respectable Rebels Threaten Somoza Dynasty," *New York Times,* 29 January 1978, E4.

4. Bernard Diederich, *Somoza and the Legacy of U.S. Involvement in Central America* (New York: E. P. Dutton, 1981), 164.

5. Ibid., 201.

6. Ibid., 205.

7. Graham Greene, *Getting to Know the General* (New York: Simon & Schuster, 1984), 187.

8. Diederich, *Somoza and the Legacy,* 217.

9. Jaime Chamorro, *La Prensa: The Republic of Paper* (New York: Freedom House, 1989), 12.

10. Diederich, *Somoza and the Legacy,* 237.

11. Ibid.

12. Ibid., 273–75.

13. Karen De Young, "U.S. Contacts Rebel Junta, Plans Food Aid to Nicaragua," *Washington Post,* 11 July 1979, A10.

14. Diederich, *Somoza and the Legacy,* 297–98.

15. Ibid., 327.

16. Charles W. Flynn and Robert E. Wilson, "An Interview with Somoza's Foe, Now Dead," *New York Times,* 13 January 1978, A23.

17. William LeoGrande, "The Revolution in Nicaragua: Another Cuba?" *Foreign Affairs* (Fall 1979): 37.

Chapter Six

1. James L. Busey, "Nicaragua and La Prensa after Somoza" (Department of Political Science, University of Colorado, Boulder, 1980), 27–28, typescript; Jaime Chamorro, *La Prensa: The Republic of Paper* (New York: Freedom House, 1989), 29.

2. Clifford Krauss, "A Contra Chief Resigns from One of His Posts," *Wall Street Journal,* 17 February 1987, 39.

3. Stephen Kinzer, "Anti-Sandinista Paper Scorns Offer," *New York Times,* 18 April 1986, A3.

4. Ibid.

5. Stephen Kinzer, "Sandinistas Are Often Tough, but the Political Debate Is Lively in Nicaragua," *New York Times,* 20 March 1986, A8.

6. Ibid.

7. Stephen Kinzer, "Nicaragua Family Saga (Cont.): A War, a Wedding," *New York Times,* 22 September 1986, L2.

8. José María Mayrink, "Violeta denuncia censura ao *La Prensa*," *O Estado de São Paulo,* 5 March 1986, 7.

9. Linda Greenhouse, "House Votes 221–209 to Aid Rebel Forces in Nicaragua; Major Victory for Reagan," *New York Times,* 26 June 1986, A1, A10; Paul Lewis, "World Court Supports Nicaragua after U.S. Rejected Judges' Role," *New York Times,* 27 June 1986, 1; Steven Kinzer, "Sandinistas Say Closed Newspaper Backed U.S.," *New York Times,* 28 June 1986, L4.

10. Violeta Barrios de Chamorro, "A Letter to Ortega," *New York Times,* 29 July 1986, A23.

Chapter Seven

1. Violeta Chamorro, "Sounds of Silence Surround La Prensa," *Times of the Americas,* 15 July 1987, 11.

2. Violeta Barrios de Chamorro, "The Death of La Prensa," *Foreign Affairs* (Winter 1986/87): 385.

3. Ibid., 385–86.

4. Chamorro, "Sounds of Silence Surround La Prensa," 11.

5. Ibid.

6. "Arias se siente optimista," *Prensa Libre* (Guatemala City), 7 June 1987, 2.

7. Philip Shenon, "Reagan Backed Inverted Values, Iran Panel Says in Tougher Draft," *New York Times,* 25 October 1987, 1, 17.

8. Paul Berman, "An Angry Peace, the Hopes and Fears of Nicaragua's Civil Opposition," *Village Voice,* 3 November 1987, 32.

9. Stephen Kinzer, "Press Curbs Remain Nicaragua Editor Charges," *New York Times,* 22 October 1987, A10.

10. Antonio Alexandre García, "La Prensa ressurge sem censura, más com límites," *Imprensa* (Rio de Janeiro) (October 1987): 34.

11. "Excerpts from Arias Talk," *New York Times,* 23 September 1987, A12.

12. Violeta Barrios de Chamorro, "Triunfó el pueblo!" *La Prensa,* 1 October 1987, 1.

13. "Editorial," *La Prensa,* 1 October 1987, 12.

14. Ibid.

15. Pablo Antonio Cuadra, "Deslindando Responsibilidades," *La Prensa,* 1 October 1987, 2.

16. "La Prensa Reopening Hailed Warily," *The Quill* 75, no. 10 (November 1987): 71.

17. Stephen Kinzer, "Nicaragua Orders U.S. Ambassador to Leave Country," *New York Times,* 12 July 1988, A10.

18. Emilio Álvarez Montalván, "What About the Nandaime 39, President Ortega?" *Wall Street Journal,* 23 September 1988, 19.

19. Michael Massing, "Nicaragua's Free-Fire Journalism," *Columbia Journalism Review* (July/August 1988): 29–35.

20. Ibid., 33.

21. Francisco Goldman, "Sad Tales of La Libertad de Prensa," *Harper's Magazine* (August 1988): 56.

22. Ibid., 62.

23. Ibid.

24. Jaime Chamorro, *La Prensa: The Republic of Paper* (New York: Freedom House, 1989), 109.

25. Stephen Kinzer, "In Nicaragua's Press, a Softer Voice," *New York Times,* 25 November 1988, A3.

26. Flora Lewis, "Violeta and Corazon," *New York Times,* 12 February 1988, A35.

27. "Protesters: Communists Get Out," *Pensacola News Journal,* 11 January 1988, A4.

28. Lewis, "Violeta and Corazon," A35.

29. "Sandinista Foes Name Candidates," *Milwaukee Journal,* 3 September 1989, A16.

30. Stephen Kinzer, "Anti-Sandinistas Choose Candidates," *New York Times,* 4 September 1989, Y1.

31. Vasily Grossman, *Life and Fate* (New York: Harper & Row, 1986), quoted in *Harper's Magazine* (March 1986): 14.

32. "Suplemento de Aniversario 10 Enero 1978 a 1985," *La Prensa,* 10 January 1985, 1 (quoted with permission).

Chapter Eight

1. David C. Korten, "Crecimiento de la Población y Calidad de la Vida en Nicaragua," Instituto Centroamericano de Administración de Empresas (INCAE), Managua, 1973, quoted by Miguel D'Escoto, Introduction to *Guardian of the Dynasty* by Richard Millett (Maryknoll, NY: Orbis Books, 1977), 9.

2. "Report of the Amnesty International Missions to the Republic of Nicaragua August, 1979, January, 1980, and August, 1980, Including Memoranda Exchanged between the Government and Amnesty International" (New York: Amnesty International, 1982).

3. Food First Action Alert, *Nicaragua: The Revolution Was the Easy Part* (San Francisco: Institute for Food and Development Policy, 1982), 1–4.

4. National Public Radio, *All Things Considered,* 25 November 1986.

5. Mario Vargas Llosa, "In Nicaragua," *New York Times Magazine,* 28 April 1985, 81.

6. Pedro Joaquín Chamorro, *Richter 7* (Managua: El Pez y la Serpiente, 1976), 145.

7. Edward Seaton, "Nicaraguan Press Law Grants New Rights to Censors," *Wall Street Journal,* 14 July 1989, A11.

8. "The Hero's Clay Feet," *Newsweek,* 15 May 1989, 32–33.

9. Aaron Epstein, "North Gets Probation, Large Fine," *Charlotte Observer,* 6 July 1989, A1.

10. Ibid.

11. Ibid., A10.

12. Jack Germond and Jules Witcover, "Light Sentence for Oliver North Will Do Little to Teach the Needed Lesson," *Pensacola News Journal,* 7 July 1989, A9.

INDEX

Index

Chamorro Barros, Carlos (*continued*) 82–83; director of *Barricada*, 82–83; PBS interview with, 82–83; "60 Minutes" interview with, 83; on social gains of revolution, 83; on U.S. aggression, 83; on brother's mistakes, 83; mother's opposition to *Barricada*, 91; on CIA aid to *La Prensa*, 98; mentioned, 48, 89, 101, 103, 112

Chamorro Barrios, Pedro Joaquín: on day of assassination, 2–3; interviews with, 68, 77–80; suspects Sandinistas, 75; disagrees with Xavier, 75–76; counterrevolutionary newspaper of, 76; exile of, 76, 81; on history of *La Prensa*, 80; with contras, 80, 83, 109; education of, 82; PBS interview with, 82

Chamorro Cardenal, Jaime: assassination theories of, 10–11; on *La Prensa* loan to Sandinistas, 68n; on Xavier's departure, 76; becomes codirector of *La Prensa*, 81; talks about Pedro Joaquín, 81; on Xavier's offer to buy *La Prensa*, 81; on the Sandinistas, 81–82; PBS interview with, 82; on U.S. assistance to *La Prensa*, 98, 102; criticizes Sandinistas, 102; Sandinista propaganda against, 103; mentioned, 3, 77, 91, 116

Chamorro Cardenal, Pedro Joaquín: assassination of, 1, 2, 3, 5, 6–7, 67, 76, 101, 109; religion of, 1, 2, 16, 34, 37, 40–41, 53, 84, 86; on end of Somoza dynasty, 2; as political leader, 2, 12, 15, 52, 61; personality of, 4, 16, 36, 49–53, 54–55, 66, 78–79, 81, 83–84, 85–88; funeral of, 4–5; predicts own death, 4–5, 12, 57–58; spurs revolution, 7–8, 10, 73, 103; theories on assassination, 8–12; letter to Somoza Debayle, 12; and Carlos Andrés Pérez, 12; exiled, 12, 15, 18, 20, 27, 32–33; ancestry of, 13, 14–15, 16; boyhood and youth of, 13, 14–15, 16, 50; on William Walker, 14; imprisoned 1944, 15; thesis of, 15; and Generation of the Forties, 15, 20; animosity with Somozas, 15, 23, 28; takes over *La Prensa*, 16; married Violeta, 16; worked with father, 16, 92; as employer 16, 49–52; on U.S. policy, 18, 119; founded UNAP, 20; and Social Democrats, 21;

and Frente Interno, 21; imprisoned 1954, 21; and plot to overthrow Somoza García, 21, 27; arrested and imprisoned 1956, 21, 22–29, 30–31, 36; and Social Christians, 21, 61, 63, 88; with Rip Van Winckle, 22; torture of, 22, 23–25, 27, 46; on Somoza power, 28; escape from San Carlos, 31–32; in Costa Rica, 32–33; organized resistance in Costa Rica, 33; asked help from Castro, 33; and 1959 rebellion, 33–36, 45, 89; letter to Violeta, 34; 1959 surrender of, 34, 36; on 1959 defeat, 34, 36; on 1959 rebellion, 35; military tribunal and 1959 imprisonment of, 35–41; dream of, 37; on despair of those who rebelled, 38; guilty of treason, 38, 39; sentence of, 39; effect of "traitor" label, 39, 40; on communism and Christianity, 40–41; on need for Christian revolution, 41; compares American ambassadors to Pilate and U.S. to Rome, 42; released in general amnesty, 43, 90; on Luís Somoza, 44; on Somoza García's newspaper, 44; radio broadcasts of, 45; literary campaign of, 45; and IAPA, 45, 63; united opposition against Somoza, 46, 61; 1967 opposition to Somoza and arrest of, 46–47; travels to Atlantic coast, 47–49; on Atlantic coast poverty and development, 48–49; and Social Security, 50; on democracy, 52; improved *La Prensa*, 52; supports Sandinistas, 53, 76; on Sandino, 53, 119; anticommunism of, 53–54, 77; criticized U.S. policies, 54–55, 84, 119; on earthquake, 55, 56, 57; on Somoza's exploitation, 57; asks Somoza to resign, 58–59, 68; on threats to country, 58–59; and group of "Twenty-seven," 59; boycott and arrest of, in 1974 elections, 59, 65; demands upon by Somoza, 60; on Sandinista hostage taking, 61; and UDEL, 61; Ernesto Cardenal on politics of, 62; disassociates from ancestors' politics, 62–63; travel restrictions on, 64; and Central American literature contest, 64; on his novels, 64 (*see also* books of); and Maria Moors Cabot Prize, 64–65; on the bourgeoisie, 65–66; criticizes Sandinistas,

136

Index

Index

Marines, U.S., 7, 16–17, 18, 53
Marxists. *See* Communists
Mayorga, Mateo, 14–15, 15n
Mollejones (Los), 34, 35, 62
Monimbó, 68
Murillo, Rosario, 77n

Nación, El, 76
Nandaime, 100
National Endowment for Democracy, 98, 102
National Guard: and Chamorroa's wake, 5; and Chamorro's assassination, 8; formation of, 18; and Sandino's murder, 18–19; and Chamorro's escape from San Carlos, 31–33; and 1959 rebellion, 34, 35, 36; killed Tomás Borge's wife, 50; and looting after earthquake, 56; after hostage taking, 60; at Monimbó, 68; at National Palace takeover, 68; during revolution, 69; at first anniversary of Chamorro's death, 70; destroys *La Prensa*, 71; abuses of, 71; kills Bill Stewart, 72; mentioned, 66, 79, 107
Nationalist Conservative Party, 45
Nationalist Liberal Party, 59
National Opposition Union, 103
National Palace, 68–69, 68n
National Security Council, 97
National Union of Popular Action (UNAP), 20
Nicaraguan Democratic Force. *See* Contras
Nicaraguan Liberal forces, 7
Nieman Foundation, 94
Nobel Peace Prize, 98
North, Oliver, 96, 97, 102, 119–21
Novedades, 63
Nuestra Frontera Recortada, 48–49
Nuevo Amanecer Cultural, 61
Nuevo Diario, El, 76, 80, 81, 82, 113

Obando y Bravo, Cardinal Miguel, 59, 73, 103, 112, 114, 116
Ocatal, 18
Olama, 34, 35, 62
Organization of American States (OAS), 45, 69, 121
Ortega, Daniel: released from prison, 60; junta member, 72; elected president, 72; inauguration of, 76–77; and Rosario

Murilo, 77n; letter from Violeta to, 92–93; visits Violeta, 97– 98; reopens *La Prensa*, 98; and 1990 elections, 103; mentioned, 100
Oxfam-America, x, 107

Padgett, John, 8–9
Paguaga Irías, Edmundo, 58
Panama, 70, 94, 117
Panama Canal, 17, 21
Pastora, Edén, 68n
Patria de Pedro, La, 45
Pérez, President Carlos Andrés, 11–12, 36, 69, 70
Pezullo, Lawrence, 72
Pierce, President Franklin, 14
Pies Descalzos de Nicaragua, Los, 47–48
Poindexter, John, 96, 97
Prensa, La: and Chamorro's wake, 5; opposition to Somozas, 9, 16, 23, 28–29; purchase of, 15; 1944 closure of, 15; 1948 reopening of, 16; Pedro Joaquín director of, 16; masthead of, 20; letter on Rip Van Winckle, 22; literacy campaign of, 45, 119; working conditions at, 49–51; essay on Sandino, 53–54; earthquake damage to, 56; reopens after earthquake, 56; on the earthquake, 56, 57 (*see also* Chamorro Cardenal, Pedro Joaquín); letter asking Somoza to resign, 58; Somoza's demands upon, 60; Chamorro's essay on the bourgeoisie, 65–66; hub of strike coordination, 67; loan to Sandinistas, 68; destruction of, 71; reopens after Somoza destroys, 71; on disappearances and executions, 71; ideological struggle within, 75, 76; Xavier's resignation, 75, 76; board of directors, 75, 76, 92; staff departed from, 76; Quinto becomes codirector, 76; Sandinista censorship of, 76, 83, 97, 98, 99; instrument of U.S. policy, 83, 98, 102; 1986 closing of, 92, 94, 95, 96, 108, 118; and World Interparliamentary Conference, 95; 1987 reopening of, 97–101 passim; newsprint from Soviet Union, 98, 101; and National Endowment for Democracy, 98, 102; challenges Sandinistas, 99–100; 15-day closing of, 100; analysis of articles, 100–102; "most fa-

Index

Index